Shame, Guilt, and Surviving Martin Bryant

*One Woman's Journey
from Terror to Joy*

KAREN COLLYER

Shame, Guilt, and Surviving Martin Bryant
One Woman's Journey from Terror to Joy
by Karen Collyer

© 2018 Karen Collyer. All rights reserved.

Published by Deep Pacific Press
305 W.Magnolia #165 Fort Collins, Colorado 80521

All rights reserved. No part of this document may be reproduced or transmitted in any form or by any means, electronic, mechanical, photocopying, recording or otherwise, or by any information storage and retrieval system, without prior written permission of Karen Collyer or publisher (except by a reviewer, who may quote brief passages and/or show brief video clips in a review).

For permissions:

Karen Collyer
karen@karencollyer.com
www.karencollyer.com

ISBN 978-1-62747-261-6 (paperback)
ISBN 978-1-62747-253-1 (eBook)

Edited by:
Karen Collyer

Cover Design by:
Karen Collyer

Trigger Warnings

As the title suggests, this memoir contains traumatic memories of the writer. If you feel emotionally triggered by anything that you read, please seek professional help to clear the trigger. One thing the writer has learned and wishes to share with you, above all else, is that sometimes you need to ask for help.

In Australia, there are a range of services you can call for help 24 hours, day or night, including Lifeline on 13 11 14.

Wherever you are, a quick Google search for emergency counselling will provide a list of possibilities for you.

Asking for, and finally being willing to accept help, has provided me with the most profound healing and growth. I wish that for you, too.

Contents

Trigger Warnings iii

The Wide-Eyed Girl, Martin Bryant and
The Port Arthur Massacre xi

Chapter 1
    Don't Ask For Help 1
Chapter 2
    Love Hurts 7
Chapter 3
    Don't Tell Nanna 11
Chapter 4
    Out of The Closet 15
Chapter 5
    Taxi 23
Chapter 6
    Who Would Believe That? 27
Chapter 7
    Expression 33
Chapter 8
    Don't Panic 39
Chapter 9
    Nowhere to Run 45
Chapter 10
    New Beginnings 51
Chapter 11
    Bad Dreams 55

Chapter 12
    Goodbye 61
Chapter 13
    Homeward 67
Chapter 14
    Past into Present.. 71
Chapter 15
    Steak, Sweat and Drugs 75
Chapter 16
    Crossing the Line 81
Chapter 17
    Cigarettes and Minties 87
Chapter 18
    Shame and Redemption 93
Chapter 19
    Betrayal.. 97
Chapter 20
    The Safe Motorbike 103
Chapter 21
    Madge 109
Chapter 22
    Ring Ring 115
Chapter 23
    Change the Record... 121
Chapter 24
    Flowers 127
Chapter 25
    Eye of the Storm 133
Chapter 26
    Stay.. 137

Chapter 27
    Adjusting 141
Chapter 28
    You Can't Tell Anyone 147

Epilogue 151

Appendix 155

When Martin Bryant's name came up in conversation I used to get so angry! Angry to the core of my being. Angry with him, angry with everyone who allowed him to get to the day, April 28, 1996, when he shot and killed thirty-five people in cold blood and injured another twenty-three. Unarmed, unsuspecting people who were simply enjoying a day out at the Port Arthur Historic Site, in Tasmania, Australia.

Imagine sitting in the sun, enjoying a light lunch, and suddenly a man walks up with a huge gun and shoots directly at you. There are some who believe Martin Bryant (let's call him Martin) didn't pull the trigger that day. They believe Martin was a patsy, that someone else dressed to look like him actually did the killing while Martin was placed at a nearby property called Seascape. Martin was eventually captured at Seascape, after he had managed to set fire to himself.

Whatever you believe, I do know he was connected to a great deal of misery, torment and death.

And it didn't start on April 28, 1996, the day of the Port Arthur Massacre.

The Wide-Eyed Girl, Martin Bryant and The Port Arthur Massacre

I believe we are all born with a certain personality, a specific set of talents and a reason for existing, which you might call your soul's purpose. Experiencing a great deal of trauma through the first twenty-eight years of my life, it has taken the next twenty for me to understand and come to terms with what I have known.

Perhaps the most important aspect in my healing has been accepting all the trauma that occurred and accepting responsibility for my part in things.

The first time my psychosomatic therapist talked to me about taking responsibility for myself I was pretty unimpressed. Why should I? I didn't ask for these things to happen to me! But as I began to explore, I began to understand for the first time the role I had played in creating and reacting to trauma in my own life.

That was the turning point. That was when I began the journey from victim to survivor. Unlike my prolonged stay in the victim space, I didn't stay long in the survivor space. Being a survivor was good for a while, but I couldn't maintain it. In that state, I was waving my banner loud and proud – I survived being molested, I survived being terrified by a stalker and so on. I had a long list of things I could proudly claim I had survived.

The next phase of my recovery was understanding that waving my survivor flag served the purpose of allowing me to give voice to my experiences, and even more so to my anger at the pain I felt. That was like an emotional tsunami! So many 'aha' moments, epiphanies. There were wonderful ones where I could say wow, I had no idea I had been so courageous there.

There were many moments that brought up my old friend shame, leaving me wishing I had done things differently, made better decisions, not hurt people along the way. Shame so powerful I buckled under its weight and almost gave up so many times.

Stepping out of survivor mode began when I started to become my own objective observer. I began not just acknowledging trauma and unpleasant memories, but also allowing myself to feel whatever arose, be that anger, sadness, humiliation, physical pain, grief.

Whatever emotions arose, the key lay in allowing myself to feel them, instead of the old habit of running away from the feeling because I absolutely believed they were more than I could ever handle. They weren't.

What I refer to as emotional tsunamis were brief, and although intensely unpleasant at times, I survived. In the moments that were so intense, mostly late at night, there was always someone available to help me through it. Facebook cops a lot of flak for being a communication killer, but for me it felt like a life-saver when a trusted friend would appear for a private chat just at the very moment I thought I could not bear it.

After every emotional tsunami, without fail, I felt so much better. Another small piece of understanding of who I am and why I behaved the way I did in particular situations would become clear.

I began to forgive myself. Having played the role of victim so well for over thirty years, it was one hell of a surprise to realise I didn't have to carry that burden anymore. I didn't have to belong to the club that made me feel so very different to everybody else. I had entered the victim club as a young child, before I had a chance to understand what it meant.

Then other traumas compounded my victim status, which I wore like an invisible cloak that hid me from view. Having taken on the victim role at such a young age, I forgot I hadn't always felt that way. By my mid-twenties I began to suspect I suffered from depression. Everyone around me seemed happier. I felt I was just pretending, so no one would notice how messed up I actually was. I also wondered if maybe everybody was just pretending, because it wasn't okay to say, "I am not okay."

In my early forties, as I continued the journey of remembering, feeling and forgiving, I was surprised at how less miserable I was starting to feel. Perhaps the most important gift I began to discover within myself was my natural sense of joy.

What follows is my explanation of how I began as a wide-eyed, curious little girl and what happened before Martin Bryant entered my life in 1988, as well as after. Understanding what happened before Martin helped me to understand why I made some of the decisions I did, why I found it so hard to get others to believe and help, and why my life was guided by the deepest feelings of shame.

This is the story of Martin Bryant, before the massacre, as I experienced him. But it is more than that. So many times I have heard people say of the abused and traumatised, why can't they "get over it," why are they so unhappy so many years post trauma? From my experience, it was because the trauma became multi, multi layered.

When I was seven, shame entered my life and discoloured everything. My emotional response to trauma from that first, profound experience, was to embody it as shame. That shame insidiously affected so many life decisions, some of them ridiculous and appalling decisions. Decisions that created further shame and regret, and the friend who always seemed to follow shame, guilt.

At the age of forty-nine, I have finally reached a place of peace within myself that allows me to observe these old friends.

As you read what occurred between Martin and me, you might wonder how I coped as well as I appeared to, why I didn't manage to get more people to believe and help me. How did I not get this man put away long before 1996, thus averting the Port Arthur Massacre?

Before Martin arrived in my life, I already believed that I was different from everyone else. I believed I was a victim of violence and shameful abuse. I believed that no one would believe me, and I believed no one would help.

What follows is my story, my truth, as I experienced it through my own senses. As you read, I ask you to consider that the aspects of my parents discussed throughout are those behaviours that played a part in trauma I experienced. As with you and I, my parents both had loving, caring, funny, intelligent and loyal parts to them too. I loved them when they lived, I love them now.

This book is not about blame. Only I can be responsible for how I feel, and I accept that. My parents, everything that happened, led me to this point. This is the point where I can acknowledge my fear, bare my soul and trust you to treat her gently, with compassion.

The terrified girl who was told, "You can't tell anyone," is finally ready to tell the world.

Chapter 1

∽ Don't Ask For Help ∾

She was a wide-eyed, golden haired, curious little girl. She looked at everything around her as exciting terrain to be explored and experienced. Early in her life she was an avid explorer. Hauling herself up over the edge of her cot at night, she would drop to the floor below, crawling off around the house to see what might entertain her.

Who knows how long she did this before the night she was found coughing furiously, locked in the kitchen where the old Kelvinator fridge had decided to let go all its gas. Nanna, ever practical, created the ingenious sleeping bag harness. It would keep her snug, contained and restrained in the cot.

She hated being constrained! Little body, little arms and legs fought that sleeping-bag creation. Lungs filled huge with air, she screamed her anguish as loudly as she could. Her screams filled the house, her despair brought tears to all, but the sleeping bag was not unzipped. No one came to offer comfort. They believed she would stop when she was too tired to scream. It never occurred to them that an essential shard of her, of her hopeful, curious nature, was being destroyed.

Another shard of her shattered the evening she was awakened by the touch of a large man. A family "friend," call him uncle, they had said. Uncles aren't supposed to hurt you, are they?

"Dad! Dad!" she called out, clutching a leather necklace in her hands. The class cool girl, who bullied her often, had made it for her. A sign that they were now friends. No more bullying. A little red leather oval with the letter 'K' carved into it, a green wooden bead on either side, hung from the necklace. As she fought and tried to scream during the rape it had broken, irreparably. She clutched it now, moaning from deep within her being as she rocked her body backward and forward.

Bed had always been a sanctuary for her, a space where she could hide, sheets pulled over her head as though she were in a universe entirely of her own making. She would read long into the night, devouring books with speed and enthusiasm. She found the feel of the pink-and-white flannel sheets comforting, enjoyed the way they changed from the initial cool welcome to warm and nurturing.

Most nights Sam the cat would be curled up with her, his head near the pillow, his plump, black haired little body between the sheets. There was not a lot of space for her in the bed, as her soft toys all had to have room under the covers too. Sam was not here this night. There was to be no witness to the invasion into her sanctuary.

She was not frightened when he entered her room. Even as he closed the door, ensuring it latched, she was not concerned. She was half asleep, in that blissful, trusting state of being, only just aware of what was happening around her.

At first he stood over her, stroking her hair from her forehead gently. Lifting the sheet, he placed a hand on her hip to roll her onto her stomach.

Before she could open her mouth to question, "uncle" had placed his strong hand firmly over her mouth. His hand was big, her mouth small. So small that the hand at times blocked her nostrils as well as her mouth.

With his other hand, he lifted her nighty and pulled down her knickers. She didn't know what to expect, didn't understand what he was doing, but she was scared.

The hand began to caress the area between her legs. She began to scream, but very little noise made it past his big hand. She wriggled and fought against him. As his hand continued to play with her genitals and explore inside her, her little body began to buck violently.

To no avail, she could not stop him. She thought it was over when he removed his fingers. Moments later he began forcing his penis into her. Saliva ran freely, choking her as she made desperate attempts to breathe.

Many times the air could not get past his hand. Her own saliva ran down into her lungs, causing her body to buck in panic even more as he thrust in and out of her.

Hot, warm liquid, a mixture of her blood and his semen, felt like it ran everywhere. Her eyes streamed, mouth gagged, spitting out saliva at every brief opportunity. The snot from her nose ran down inside her throat, making breathing even more difficult.

Just when she thought she might die, he stopped.

As she lay gagging he pulled up her knickers, pulled her nightie back down and sat on the bed beside her. After pulling her bedding back up over her, covering her right to her chin, he patted her in the same way a loving father might console his beloved daughter.

When he turned her head so she had to look at him, he held a finger to his lips, shook his head from side to side, "Don't tell your mother, you can't tell anyone," he said. And then he stood up and left the room.

She did not fully understand what had happened. Whatever it was he had done, it hurt, burning. It hurt, so much, and she felt ashamed. At first, she did not dare move. Her head throbbed, chest felt as though it might explode.

She lay quite still, breathing fast, crying. Then rolling onto her side, knees clutched to her chest, she began rocking back and forth, back and forth. As the rhythm built so did her anguish. The tears ran fast, breathing became laboured as her terror, pain, and grief found a way out of her body and she began screaming.

"Daddy, help! Daddy, help!"

She was nearly seven years of age now. Her golden curls had turned to straight brown hair, but she still had huge, inquiring green eyes. The green eyes were almost black with anguish as she nursed herself and screamed, "Daddeeeeeeee!"

Dad did not come. Her screams subsided to quiet moans as she continued to rock her little body, calling quietly for help. From the other end of the house, over the sound of loud adult voices and loud music, he could not hear her. When he finally did come, it was not to help her. Her desperate calling out had sparked a rage in him.

Hearing him enter her room, his familiar belching sound with him, she had rolled onto her back. Whack! Uncontrollable, violent and swift. The comfort and protection she had called for came in the form of his fist slamming down hard across her chest.

Her father, intoxicated and enraged by the noise she was making, hit her with all his might across the chest. He hit her again, harder. And again. He hit so hard she stopped breathing. The wide-eyed, curious little girl left her body.

Looking down at the scene from above, she was not scared. She was happy to be out of the body that hurt, bled, and felt so terribly ashamed. It felt good to be light, free. No one could even see her up here, never mind interfere with her.

Her mother appeared, screaming at her father, at the uncle and aunt who were now in the room.

"She's not breathing," screamed her mother. "What have you done?" she roared at the father. The uncle and aunt stepped back. Mum wailed, looking up to the ceiling where her wide-eyed curious little girl hovered. Feeling for the heartbeat, she then hit the wide-eyed girl's chest hard and gave a few quick breaths.

What a strange feeling it was for the wide-eyed girl as she felt herself back in her body. Her lungs heaved as they filled with air, desperate to breathe.

Her mother held her, rocked her and sobbed uncontrollably for some time.

"We should call the police," the aunt insisted.

"No!" Uncle said firmly, "we don't need them interfering. What would happen to him?" Uncle asked, while nodding toward Dad.

Mum held the wide-eyed girl, calming them both as she rocked the little body gently with hers. The others quietly left the room. Mum did not pull back the sheets, nor ask any questions. Nothing was ever asked, nothing was said. Sober Dad would not remember, and Mum would not remind him, for she would not wish to wake that beast and suffer his temper.

The shame for the wide-eyed girl was so great that she never said a word, she didn't know how. Her eyes were closed now, curiosity dulled.

She understood fear now in its most intense form. But it wasn't what you might be expecting. She wasn't afraid of dying, but of the physical pain she had endured and the grief it caused her mother. She had enjoyed being free from her body.

In that flesh-tearing rape by her "uncle" and the belting that followed from her father, she understood what men were capable of. It terrified her.

The rape, her father's violent response and the silence that followed, thrust her into a world of terrifying isolation. A world where she did not dare ask for help.

Chapter 2

∽ Love Hurts ∾

It took some time for her body to heal. She dreaded visits to the bathroom, putting it off every time until she was ready to burst. Even her mother telling her stories of little girls who died because they held on to their wee until their kidneys burst didn't encourage her to go more often.

She could not, because the pain was unbearable and every time she felt the pain she felt the shame. She knew no one loved her now. No one could, not now that she had been made into this disgusting version of herself. She would sooner die than ever be found out.

It was her fault. How else could it be? But she understood that it was a monstrous failing in the uncle, that something inside him allowed him to do terrible, disgusting things to her that other men would not even think of. Would they?

This is what she wrote, many years later:

My father wronged me. For the first ten years of my life he chastised me so harshly. He created so much fear, loathing and disgust for me, my mother and my siblings. Fear should, you might think, have shut me up. When Dad hit, he hit hard, far too hard for the body of a small child. Sometimes the pain would remain for hours. I was left sobbing, alone in my room crying repeatedly, "Mummy! Mummy!"

But she never came. He hit, she left me hurt and terrified. Vulnerable, alone. Shocked. Such brutality for no reason. Sometimes, many times, it was simply because my presence, my voice, annoyed him. He would go from calm and relaxed to red-faced and spitting with rage in a moment. So fast. So unpredictable.

I learned to move fast, run out the front door, down the street, hide behind a car in a neighbour's drive. For all my hiding, I'm not sure he ever came out the front door after me. It was as though the entrance to the house was an invisible barrier that stopped him. Most times I didn't make it to the door.

He would rage in front of me, his bright red face beaded with sweat, pushed so close to mine I dared not breathe for I did not wish to breathe in his foul breath. His breath didn't smell in the tangible, physical sense, but it felt warm and foul, full of his rage and self-disgust. He would open his mouth and bellow, "Shut the fuck up! I can't stand the sound of your horrible voice!"

Then Dad would hit, hard, around the head or around the bum, as hard as he could.

Rage expressed, he would turn and walk back to the loungeroom, his domain, back to his beer and television. He succeeded in shutting down my voice. Not so much physically, but in my confidence.

Once, in a drunken stupor, he expressed to teenage me his belief that I may have been his brother's child, not his.

"Your mother, she couldn't resist him," Dad had spluttered. I never found out if there was any truth to this. He never mentioned it sober and I never asked. Asking Mum once, her response was to laugh loudly and say, "I wish!"

I had big dreams. I wanted to be a vet, to make a difference for animals in the world. But my confidence was so shattered I struggled to make friends, struggled to believe anyone would want to be friends with me or I could ever hope to create anything I truly desired. Ironically, when I overcame this to study radio and become a radio announcer, Dad was *one of my proudest fans. Later in my adult life Dad supported me unreservedly and encouraged others to do the same.*

There were profound effects from the early abuse. But Dad also taught me that I am able to forgive, to love people as they are, as faulty and difficult as they can sometimes be. I learned from Dad that the way a person is in this moment isn't necessarily who they will always be. By forgiving Dad and allowing him to show me his gentler side, I was able to let go of my fear and resentment of him and finally get to know him a little.

Things improved for a bit when she started high school, age twelve. Her father had finally conceded defeat and left the family home for good. She came home from school to find her father packed and ready to go. His explanation was brief and his exit fast. Wide-eyed girl cooked a chocolate cake to celebrate. Mum and her brother joined in, but not her sister. Dad had always adored and favoured her sister, so his leaving hit her hard at first. Things were good for a while, calm. No more arguing, no more of the sarcastic, passive-aggressive communication between Mum and Dad.

And then the holiday was over.

Mum met the first post-marriage boyfriend. A pervert. He was fascinated with the developing bodies of the wide-eyed girl and her sister, who was a year older than she. He wasn't too kind to their sweet younger brother either, being overly keen to lay a punch or a kick his way.

Mum was so blinkered by her love for him, her excitement that someone might actually be interested in her, love her even, that she could not imagine the kind of man he truly was. Leaving him to babysit the children some evenings, she did not accept their claims that he had interfered with them in her absence.

"He touches our breasts Mum, touches our bums, it's horrible."

The girls were scared. How far would he go? The wide-eyed girl knew how far he could go, dimly in her memory she understood. Her shame and fear rose like a terrifying wave that threatened to drown her every time he leered at her, said something inappropriate about her body, or touched her where he shouldn't have.

Mum did nothing to stop him when he would jump up from the dinner table to hit her or her brother. The mother who showed so little emotion physically, who rarely even cuddled her children, was suddenly comfortable sitting on the boyfriend's lap at the dinner table, kissing and allowing him to fondle her breasts in front of her children.

After many months, when the children had put up with as much violence, molestation and open threats of sexual abuse as they could manage, they confronted their mother.

"It's us or him," they demanded. She chose them, at least verbally. But something in her changed, something broke, and she responded in her despair by breaking down into a barely functional version of herself.

Mum tore the kitchen apart, grabbing at anything, saucepans, crockery, and knives flying through the air. She screamed, red-faced, determined that she should not live another moment of this god-awful life. The kids called Dad to come and get them. The last person she would want to see, but where else could they go? They called Nanna, too. Then they waited. The raging in the kitchen continued as the children left with their father, safe in their belief that Nanna would know what to do.

Emotional shock left them quiet and shaken. The wide-eyed girl continued to shake for some time.

Years later, Nanna described walking into the kitchen that day. She had waited, calmly and patiently, for their mother's frantic expression to stop. Then her arms opened as her daughter stepped into her embrace and her heartache poured out in huge, breathtaking sobs. Together they slid to the floor, where Nanna held her, stroked her hair and waited for the storm to pass.

Chapter 3

❧ Don't Tell Nanna ❧

"Who's going to want me now, with three lousy kids?" Mum would lament loudly, each day, during her morning shower. Her wailing could be heard throughout the house. The three lousy kids were scared. The enormity of Mum's emotions was frightening and unpleasant. She would stomp around the house, crying, complaining about men, about the kids. And every now and then she would devise a plan to end her pain.

The pervert had given Mum an expensive push bike, a beautiful shade of shimmery pink. That was her first inspiration. Mum got on that bike one afternoon and rode to the bridge that joins the eastern and western shores of Hobart. She might have gone ahead with her plan to jump to her death in the cold waters below, but she never made it to the top of the bridge. Somehow Mum managed to crash the bike into the railings, get tangled, and give up. By the time she returned home to complain to the kids of her failure, the bruises had already begun to show.

She didn't ride again. Instead she visited the family doctor. Sleeping tablets were prescribed. Perhaps if she could sleep she would start to feel better. Perhaps – or she might just swallow half a bottle of the tablets one night and see if that would end it.

It didn't. But it did scare the hell out of the wide-eyed girl's older sister and her friends. They had been enjoying a sleepout in the cubby house out back. The girls were well into their evening, having enjoyed a bottle of spirits, wine and cigarettes, when a ghostly apparition appeared.

No one would ever forget the sight of Mum in her pink nighty with the squirrel on it, staggering, crying. The sisters managed to get her into bed. Scouring the room, they removed the sleeping pills and swore at the doctor for prescribing them. Couldn't he see how depressed she was?

The sisters went to Nanna's, where the wide-eyed girl stayed on and off for the best part of a year, and for the next five years was a frequent visitor. Arriving at their Nanna's, the girls were initially relieved. Safe at last!

Their relief was short lived. Their grandfather (by marriage, not genetic) soon took a shine to them both, taking it upon himself to wake them early on school mornings.

"Do you know how lucky you are?" he'd say as he sat on the edge of the bed, clumsy big hands fumbling under the sheet in their search for growing young breasts. He loved to land his slobbery mouth on a nipple, have a good suck and then move on to the other sister. It was such a shock neither knew what to do. The wide-eyed curious one did, though. She asked for an alarm clock, so as to not have to wake Nanna and her husband each morning. Nanna of course agreed, she would have done anything for her beautiful girls.

Wide-eyed girl experimented, until she found a time that was early enough to beat the old bastard. The girls would get up, get showered, dressed and ready, then wait in the kitchen for Nanna. Often on her own, as her sister spent days at a time at her best friend's, the wide-eyed girl would return from her shower and place a heavy box on the door to their room. This worked well, as their room was an attic above the kitchen.

The old bastard couldn't get the lid open with the box on it. Some days she would wake to hear him grunting with the effort of trying to open the door. The beauty of it was there was nothing he could do about it. What could he say? She would wait a few minutes after he stopped trying, then open the door and dart down to the bathroom, shower, and dart back up the stairs. She felt so much more vulnerable on her own, which was most of the time. When she heard Nanna in the kitchen she would come down, bright and bubbly as though everything was wonderful.

As they got older the girls stayed in the downstairs bedroom. Much easier to avoid the old bastard. Nanna's bedroom was on the other side of the wall. All she had to do was talk loudly to put him off. From this room she missed the view of the ocean at night, the sound of the water and the breeze, but she traded that for safety.

They could have told Nanna. Had they been adult they would have. But they had just witnessed their mother's drawn-out mental breakdown and were recovering from the terror of that. The wide-eyed girl now knew not only what men were capable of, but that knowing it could destroy the women they loved.

So this time, instead of telling the truth, they worked around it. Sometimes they won, sometimes they didn't, but they never let Nanna know and they protected her with all their might.

Chapter 4

❧ Out of The Closet ❦

Apart from Nanna and her siblings, the most powerful survival tool she had was music. The first record she bought, 'Changes One Bowie,' began her lifelong love of David Bowie's music. Bowie's song 'Heroes' lifted her spirits, and helped her get dressed and go to school, even though she felt incredibly miserable and out of place when she got there.

Going to a "private school for young ladies" when her family was very poor and she felt alienated and ashamed was no walk in the park. In the morning, Cold Chisel's song 'Choir Girl,' played very loud, always got her body dancing. Bono and U2's haunting 'With or Without You' helped her emotions to release, tears flowing, at the end of a bad day. Volume as loud as it could go without ruining the speakers, she would open her mouth wide and sing along with absolute gusto. It felt as though Bono knew exactly how she was feeling and had written the song especially for her. As the song ended she would wrap her arms around her body, hug herself tight, and imagine what it might feel like to be safe.

During her last year of high school, the wide-eyed girl found love. He was in his early twenties, she was only seventeen. Scandalous! That's what her mother said. This young man took up a lot of her time. At one point he even suggested marriage. The wide-eyed girl was smitten. She hadn't experienced the delicious joy of being truly cherished before. At first she was a little wary, was he really as good as he seemed? But he was.

He knew she studied hard, so while her mother's imagination created a fantastic range of appalling situations and behaviours her daughter might be engaged in with this man, the reality was very, very different. Many evenings he spent simply providing food and cups of coffee while she worked on her homework. He had not achieved higher education then, but valued it highly and encouraged her with such sincerity.

"You'll end up pregnant, broke, and stuck in a shit house with this loser!" her mother screamed one morning, then the next morning, and the next.

"Perhaps," the wide-eyed girl eventually replied, "but that would have to be better than living here with you!"

Mother and daughter faced each other from either end of the short hallway. It was a cool morning, the cold seeping up through the floorboards and the cheap, thin carpet that did little to protect them. Mum's face went a deep, deep shade of red, her flesh wobbling as her rage exploded.

"You ungrateful little bitch!" she screamed as she flew at her daughter. For the first time in the girl's seventeen years, her mother's hand slammed hard across her face, snapping her head backwards and sideways. Before she had time to think, the wide-eyed girl responded, hitting back.

In that moment, everything changed. The energy that had built up between them was gone, replaced by a hollow sorrow.

Convinced she must save her daughter from this relationship, Mum contacted the headmaster of the private school and painted a pretty grim picture. When the wide-eyed girl was called into his office soon after, she was too shocked and humiliated to defend herself.

The sexual acts her mother had accused her of surprised even her. None of it was real, but the headmaster hadn't called her in to hear her side of things, rather to describe to her the punishments he would enact immediately. No longer would she be free to study in the common room with the other final-year students when she had a free session. Every free lesson for her would now be spent in the library, under the strict supervision of the librarian. Her body shook with anger, frustration, hurt and humiliation.

As her hand wandered to her face, still bruised and tingling from the impact of her mother's hand, silent tears fell. It didn't matter what she did, how hard she studied, she would never be accepted. Not by Mum, not by this school. She would simply never be good enough. The injustice of her situation hit her hard. She should pack her things and run. When she threatened to do that Mum had promised to call the police, to have her boyfriend charged. Could she do that? It would be different once she was eighteen.

As she settled into a sunny corner in the library, having endured the well-intended but humbling explanation from the librarian of what was expected of her during this time, her mind raced, searching for alternatives. Knees pulled up under her chin, she closed herself off in defence. Word of her humiliation had already spread. As she gathered books from her locker in the common room she endured knowing looks, and heard the words slut and tart. Unbidden tears fell fast. She felt so unsafe, unwelcome, unloved.

Within two days everything changed again, once more without her consent. Only this time she was relieved. Unbeknown to her, Nanna stepped in and convinced Mum to send her to Melbourne for a while, to stay with Mum's sister. Torn between excitement at the prospect of spending time with the aunt she adored and sorrow at being separate from the boyfriend, she had no choice but to pack a bag and do as she was told.

Mum had been right in one aspect, for she had begun to have a sexual relationship with her boyfriend. Their first time together she had been nervous, not sure what to expect. Although she could not recall it, her previous experience, locked deep down in the basement of her subconscious, had been hellish, forced upon her. She tried to relax, but it was impossible. She was terrified, waiting for the pain.

He was loving and gentle, but did not know of her past. This felt so different, physically and emotionally, from the pain she had anticipated. In that moment of realisation, she was overwhelmed with horror. She understood now what had happened when she was younger. She still had no access to the memory, but she knew she had been assaulted, but not in the same way. If only she could remember!

Keeping all of this to herself, she went home quietly, consumed by the disgust she felt. Her body felt irritated, as though every nerve in her being was screaming, "No, no, no!" and firing off in dramatic response to the memory that had yet to reveal itself.

Yet she told him none of this, simply put on her "game face" and pretended everything was wonderful. She could not bear to consider, explore and accept the truth for herself. The disgust and shame she felt was so great she could not give it language. And if she told him, what then? Would he believe her? Would he feel as disgusted by her as she did of herself? She believed he would, because she did, and it tainted everything.

During the three months she spent in Melbourne she maintained contact with the boyfriend, until she finally conceded to her mother's demand that she break things off with him. She would not be allowed to return home until she did. She considered refusing to go home, even went for a job interview and was offered a secretarial job. But the pull of home won.

What she didn't know then, was that the boyfriend's mother worked with abused children and was in a position to help. Interesting though, even years later as she writes this, the wide-eyed girl recognised that she was more afraid of being placed in a system that was full of unknowns and possibly more dangerous living situations than those she had already survived, so the mother's help would not have been welcome.

She knew now too that as difficult as family life had been, she had not wanted to leave, for it was all she knew.

Apart from the old bastard, there were no outwardly abusive men after that. At the end of 1986, aged eighteen, wide-eyed girl finished school, wanting more than anything to go to university and become a Veterinary Surgeon. She was smart enough, keen enough, but she knew so little of the world, and what she did know was so awful, that when her mother told her she could not go because the family could not afford it, she believed her. Swallowing her disappointment, she went into nursing instead. She loved nursing! She could love and care for people, being smart was finally rewarded: she felt like she could fit in.

But then one afternoon the old bastard visited her mother's to cut the lawn, as he often did. Asleep in her bed, she heard his car pull up, heard him let himself in the front door. Vulnerable and alone, she jumped out of bed, pulled the covers up so the bed looked made, and climbed into her wardrobe. She stayed there, silently, until she heard his car pull away nearly two hours later. Shaking, she phoned the student nurses' home, explained what had happened and her history with the old bastard, and was granted a room that day.

That was the last time she felt part of a family, that she had a home to go to. She packed while she waited for her mother to come home from work. Telling her mother over dinner, she did her best to explain why. But her mother was heart-broken and attacked her, offering no care or support at all. Did her mother hear her? Probably not.

The boyfriend at the time, a platonic relationship, arrived to collect the girl and her few bags and take her to the nurses' home. He ran for his life as her mother chased them both out of the house, across the yard and into the street.

Wide-eyed girl was inconsolable. She understood she would not be able to go back. How long would it be before her mother understood and would love her? With all this pouring out of her in huge sobs, the wide-eyed girl was left standing on the footpath outside the nurses' home, as her boyfriend abruptly ended their relationship.

"I'm sorry," he blurted hastily, "this is too much for me. I don't want to see you again. Please don't call." He turned, walked to his car without looking back, climbed in and was gone.

The wide-eyed girl, once curious but now dulled again, found herself in a small room with a cold tiled floor, a single bed, desk, lamp and a small wardrobe. Never in her life had she felt more alone, less loved or less valued. How would she live in this desolate space? Once her tears had dried and her bladder was screaming so loudly she could no longer ignore the call to urinate, she left the safety of her cold room to explore her surrounds.

Opposite her was a large shower room. A row of showers and a row of sinks. Pretty old, completely lacking in comfort or charm, but functional. Toilets in the room next door. A few doors down on her side of the corridor was the lounge room.

Lounge sounds comfortable, inviting, right? Wrong. Still a tiled floor, grey and light, lime green, most unappealing to the wide-eyed girl. This room had a dozen or so vinyl armchairs that if you sat in for more than five minutes made your ass sweat. There was a kettle, a toaster, a never-ending supply of toast, butter and jam, tea, coffee and milk.

The move, her arrival, and the coldness of this place was such a shock. She continued to turn up to training and to work, but she ached with a loneliness that she could feel throughout her body. During the day, she managed to hold back the tears, but on her own at night in that lonely room the tears seemed to last forever.

Surviving the loneliness of the nurses' quarters, so foreign after life in a busy home with her brother and sister, her cats, dog, and television to watch, was hard. She hadn't been there long when her brother phoned to say the dog and one of the cats had been poisoned and had passed away. This was devastating news, and the last straw.

One night she climbed the stairs to the top of the building, hoping she had the courage to jump and set herself free. Oh, disappointment! Looking down over the edge, she felt sure the building was not actually high enough. All she was likely to achieve was serious damage to her physical body. Life was pretty tough just now, but life stuck in a hospital bed in a body that no longer worked for itself would be far, far worse.

Connectedness is like the holy grail of human existence. Those who don't have it can't imagine how incredibly beautiful it feels, but they seek it, they want it. They just know they are not complete.

Searching, always searching, always wanting more. More connection, more purpose, more reason for being alive. It was never about money and things for you. You enjoy things, a little like a magpie, because they remind you of people, emotions, of being loved, even for a moment.

As you remember more, as you become stronger in your divine truth, your ability to see, you will need fewer mementos. For everything is available to you, even in your darkest moments when you feel disconnected. Like when you are in the void. You used to feel so alone, so helpless, so without love or hope. And yet you are not. You are part of everything, how could you ever really be alone?

Chapter 5

∽ Taxi ∾

At the age of eighteen all she knew of men was that they took what they wanted. Sex was what they wanted, not love, not intelligence, not conversation. They took all those things in like a sponge, but underneath all they really wanted was sex. How do you conduct a relationship with men? Give them what they want, frequently, and yet even that didn't work. She wasn't aware she was doing this. She was not really aware at all, believing what she was experiencing was normal. Yet she was beginning to understand that relationship might not be about sex, that she needed to develop better relationships that were about who she was, not what she had to offer.

As she began to understand this and believe in herself just a little more, she made friends, mainly men, who did value her as she was. And then she accepted a dinner invitation. He was an interesting character, a man who liked fashion, art, and had a strange walk due to an injury many years ago. She knew him from the nightclub she frequented. Her friends all knew him, so she felt safe accepting his invitation, although she suspected he was also keen on her best friend.

She hadn't been asked to dinner often, and felt butterflies in her stomach as she prepared. Tweed mini skirt and matching jacket, with black jumper underneath and a fantastic gothic silver cross, complete with the body of the Christ on it. Silver hoop earrings, deep red lipstick, and she was ready.

When she arrived he was waiting at the door, all gentlemanly manners. Opening the door, he bowed, sweeping his arm towards the hallway behind to beckon her in. He had cooked, nothing extraordinary, but he seemed proud of his efforts.

Dinner complete, he asked her to follow him.

"I have some fabric that would look good on you," he said, "a skirt perhaps." His hand gently stroked her leg. She wasn't sure how she felt about that. By now she realised he was leading her into his bedroom. Before she could protest he had pushed her onto the bed.

"No, no, I don't think so," she responded.

He ignored her, pushing himself on top of her. She froze, not knowing what to do. He began to explore her body, first with his eyes, then more clumsily with his hands.

"No, no!" she kept saying. Eventually he stopped, but did not move from her. Every time she tried to move, his hands grabbed her wrists and pinned her down. He smiled, laughed, as he restrained her, but it was not funny.

She struggled and fought to free herself. Several times he relaxed his hold on her, allowing her to sit up, before pushing her back down again. He was taller and much stronger than she, so she was unlikely to stop him by physical means. He was on top of her, using his legs to hold her, his hands still pinning her wrists to the bed. Talking, that was it. She started talking, and kept going, until he rolled off her and lay on the bed looking exasperated.

"You know if you keep doing this, it's rape. There's no way I am going to go out with you if you do this. What kind of relationship is built on that? Wouldn't you rather we were friends first?" He seemed to be considering this. Then her chance came when he asked did she want coffee?

"Yes, please," she replied.

He disappeared into the kitchen, she to the hallway where the phone was. Picking it up, she dialled the number for a taxi, and gave the address before the phone was yanked out of her hand. Pulling the cord from the wall, he wrapped it around the phone before placing it in the nearby cupboard, locking the door, and slipping the key into his pocket.

"Where do you think you're going?" he menaced.

"Home," she whimpered, although it was hard to speak, her voice seemed small and tight. He grabbed her arms. She fought for her life, pushing against him. For a moment she was free. She made it to the front door, yanking it open before charging outside.

He grabbed her from behind, big arms held firmly around her, lifting her feet off the ground. Screaming as loudly as she could, she fought him, wriggling with all her might. Angered, he tipped her upside down, dropping her head first on the solid concrete path.

Dazed, she lay still for a moment, unsure what to do next. She was dimly aware of his footsteps retreating. A car had pulled up. As she got to her feet a male voice reached her.

"You called for a taxi?"

Chapter 6

 Who Would Believe That?

The next day she hurt in so many places. After her shower she noticed dark bruises on her arms, wrists and legs. Her head and neck hurt badly. She took a few pain killers and went to work.

"What happened to you?" the nurse in charge asked. "Should you be home in bed?"

"I'm okay," she replied, "it was an accident, nothing broken." Physically perhaps, but another shard of her had been torn off, smashed onto the concrete. The last thing she could bear was a day completely alone in her room to go over and over what had happened. As she went about her work over the following weeks her ability to deal with patient trauma grew less and less. She became obsessed with the possibility of death. Would he have killed her that night? Or would he have settled for raping her?

"Nothing actually happened," her girlfriend told her, "he didn't rape you."

"But he hurt me! I was so scared, you saw the bruises!" Once more the wide-eyed girl realised she was alone. None of her friends wanted to hear what had happened, it wasn't at all convenient. After all, he was a friend too. So where did that leave her? Ashamed once more and questioning herself. She could imagine what Mum's reaction would have been, don't exaggerate, you do like to exaggerate. But she wasn't exaggerating. It had happened to her.

Yes, she wanted people to believe her, to take her side. She wanted someone to take a stand for her. But no one did. For months after, every time she saw the man, in the street, at a nightclub, he would come close, too close. Leaning over her, establishing his power over her, he would bend down and snarl right in her face, "Are you still telling people about how I attacked you?" He seemed angry that she had told their friends, yet enjoyed gloating over her inability to be believed.

Sometimes he grabbed her by the wrist as he leaned in, holding so tight it hurt her. She wanted to hit out, retaliate, but he was so much bigger and was always quick to hold her tight in a way that hurt her, reminding her that he had all the power. To complicate things even more, her closest friend began dating the man.

"Don't be selfish," she was told, "we are in love."

Selfish – the unforgivable crime! Being selfish is bloody dangerous. It means listening to your voice, not to the others. It means you might just get close to realising there is a key within you to the truth you have forgotten. The truth that never left. The pure, unadulterated truth of who you are and the incredible stories you could share if only you could remember.

The unlocking begins, even though you don't realise that is what is happening.

You are one of the lucky ones. You reached that point of crisis, of self-loathing deep enough to want to give up, to be free of this body once and for all. And something changed. Your life turned upside down, like a tsunami had been invited in. It was raw, unpleasant, it cost you a lot that you held dear. But it gave you more, so much more.

The waters rose high and you drank in much of it, choking, drowning, losing the strength to keep swimming. But you did keep swimming and here you are now.

Holding the key in your hand, you stand on the edge of discovery. Your breath is short and shallow. There is excitement, fear, joy and expectation all mingled together in a delightful cocktail of anticipation.

Turn the key in your hand. Feel its smooth, brassy texture. Once you put the key in the lock and turn it there is no going back. You cannot put this genie back in the bottle. Life will change. Hesitation comes from understanding that once you turn the key much of what you "believe" will become redundant.

Your concepts of life, time, relationships, beliefs, death, birth, loss - everything will change and there is no going back. Once you know, you cannot un-know. Sit for a while. Feel the warm power of mother earth. Smell the damp, earthy aromas coming from the freshly watered garden. Hear the waves crash on the ocean.

You feel the vastness of the universe, of nature, of these elements that keep on going as human life comes and goes. Your human life will come and go. What are you afraid of? Hold the key a little longer if you wish. Don't let it go.

Sometime later she took what for her was a brave leap and moved into a room in a shared house. This was only marginally less lonely, but she had more room, access to a television and bath and there was a dog to play with. By now she had a new boyfriend. It wasn't well-balanced though. For while she thought it was true love and monogamous, he was not restricting his romantic relations to her. They lived in a fairly small town, so inevitably she found out about this, and once more the black hole of loneliness threatened to eat her alive.

If only she had known then that a relationship can't be built where there is no trust. The relationship with this man continued, on and off, over the next few years. In the end, although she had loved him so much, the wide-eyed girl felt he had not been trustworthy, that he had betrayed her.

It was not until her healing began more than twenty years later, in her early forties, that she finally understood that she was the one with the trust issues. Relationships cannot flourish without trust, of self and others, or without open communication. What she had wanted was to feel safe, for him to see all her pain, to take it away and make her feel better. She learned later, though, that she was the one who must learn how to do that. As she began to understand this, she was able to look back on their time together with immense gratitude for his companionship, for walking beside her and loving her as best he could.

Things got a bit unpleasant as the romantic relationship between the couple with whom she shared the house began to fall apart. This time she moved to a flat in the city, above a fast food shop, just across the road from a public radio station. She hadn't had much to do with radio, but she loved music. She went out dancing until all hours several nights a week, drinking enough vodka to dampen her loneliness and free her body to move with more grace than she was accustomed to.

She felt so ashamed still, different from everybody else. She was sure wherever she went people could see she didn't belong, could see her shame and judged her for it.

She left her nursing training after weeks of deliberating over why she could not bear to nurse people to their death. Death wasn't something she had dealt with yet in her life, and she had all but forgotten the terrible night of abuse that had resulted in her leaving her body. She had forgotten that death wasn't unpleasant, scary or awful. She was terrified of death.

She remembered with great emotion the many times, as a small child, she had been convinced today was the day she and her siblings would die at their father's hand. He was verbally and sometimes physically violent, but he would never have killed them intentionally. But Dad was an alcoholic. A car-driving alcoholic, whose wife was too scared to drive a car.

The problems began when the bridge connecting Hobart's eastern and western shores lost a section after the ship, Lake Illawarra, smashed into it in 1975. This meant the bus that normally took Mum to work on the other side of the river wasn't running, as the bridge was unusable. Dad had to drive her to the barge that crossed the river instead.

Clutching her seatbelt, the little six-year-old would try not to cry or scream as Dad drove the car way too close to the edge of the road, where the land disappeared into the dark water. Or when he careered through stop lights, not noticing the traffic stopping all around to let him through. She didn't want to do anything that would take his attention off driving.

She imagined what it would be like to be dead. There would be no Mum, no Nanna, no animals. She would be alone. Terrified, each day she clutched her seatbelt, cried as silently as she could, and prayed to a God she was not sure existed. So now, at age nineteen, bruised and afraid, she was once more horrifyingly aware of the possibility of death and it was more than she could face.

How much time have you spent in this life fearing your death? Is the real fear the knowing that you must do it alone? Regardless of who or how many stand with you as you die, you have no choice but to travel alone and face it alone. You are getting closer to understanding death as a transition. Almost like changing clothes. Out of one suit and into another.

But it hasn't always been like this. Death loomed through your life as a terrifying prospect, tragic destroyer of hope, taking away forever those you loved. Cruel, terrible death. And now, as you become less fearful, you smile, remembering the first time you were able to hear and converse with one who had died, one who had gone, and yet here they were.

Yes, you still mourn the physical loss, no longer can you cuddle and feel them close, feel the familiar tone of their voice. But their essence is never far, and this gives you great comfort. There is much room for growth here, but you understand that and it's okay.

Death brings great change, which isn't easy for most. You struggle, afraid of what you don't know, what you can't imagine. What if the things you can't imagine are more magnificent than anything you have ever experienced or dreamed of? What if that truth about you is so incredible, so loving, gentle, strong, powerful and present, absolutely present, and because you are too scared to really live you rob yourself of ever experiencing that?

She quit, traded her fob watch for a microphone, and began learning how to talk live on air on the public radio station across the road from her home.

Chapter 7

 Expression

1988

Wide-eyed girl was wide-eyed indeed! Radio announcing was exhilarating! There was a big room full of vinyl records, and before a show she got to choose whatever music she wanted to play! Freedom! Expression! As a little girl she had been shut down so much.

"Shut the fuck up Karen! I can't stand the sound of your fucking voice!" her father had drunkenly roared at her so many times, shattering her happiness in a moment.

"Shut the fuck up!"

Not anymore! With the microphone in front of her, news coming in 24/7, she became politically engaged. Stories of massacre, poverty and cruelty got her on her feet asking why? She asked her audience why. She found music to match the news, to match how she felt in response to the news. She found music that expressed her joy in being alive, her joy in being able to turn the sound up wall-shatteringly loud and dance around the studio.

This was a busy time, as she also applied for jobs constantly. It wasn't easy living on welfare. But she was rarely invited to an interview, never mind offered a job. She survived partly due to the generosity and compassion of friends and her sister. Just when she needed it most a box of food would arrive, or a new piece of clothing.

She found peace in the loud music, in the expression and in the incredible acceptance and encouragement she received from the other volunteers at the radio station. This was new, so new! She had never been accepted anywhere, just as she was.

Like the father who tried to shut her down, in came the Stalker.

"You sound so sexy when you talk," he said, the first time he called. One a.m., alone in the studio, wide-eyed girl felt a chill down her spine. There was something that didn't feel good about this caller. His voice was a little odd, his tone not quite nice.

"What are you wearing?" he enquired. She didn't reply, didn't understand his meaning.

"Are you wearing underwear?" he continued. Oh God it's a creep! She didn't hang up the phone straight away. Something about him frightened her. Her hands didn't move to hit the disconnect button. She had learned to freeze when she was afraid, and that's what happened now.

"My friend, she is quite old, she wears big panties, they dry on the line and I think they are quite nice. Do you wear pants like that?" he asked.

Finally, her body unfroze and she hit the disconnect button. She felt ashamed, as though all the world knew she had behaved badly, had been a bad, disgusting girl. Putting another record on, she ran for the washroom to wash her face, wash her hands and feel clean.

She felt so ashamed still, different to everybody else. She was sure wherever she went people could see she didn't belong, could see her shame and judge her for it.

It would be nearly thirty years later that she finally began to understand her shame and where it had begun.

I was born into shame. My mother's shame. She had been raised to be polite, well-mannered and considerate. Mum was proud of her teenage years at one of Hobart's most prestigious schools for "young ladies." But her heart was so darkened by shame. She was already engaged to my father when she realised she was pregnant, but I wonder if they would have gone ahead with the marriage had they not felt they had to.

Dad was quite vulgar in his behaviour, compared to Mum. He used language she did not like, walked around the house in his underwear, freely grabbing his balls for a scratch and a readjustment without worrying about who could see him. Mum would sneer at him in response, cringing away from him.

Dad was working as a taxi driver when I was born. He worked hard, cleaning during the day, driving by night, to support Mum and my older sister. Unfortunately, he fell into bad habits, drinking heavily and regularly with his driving buddies before returning home to Mum. She didn't feel supported, even though he was doing what he did for her. His drunken antics were legendary, but not in a good way.

One of my earliest memories of Dad is him coming home drunk and taking the meal Mum had saved for him, served up on a china plate, and hurling it at a wall with all his might.

He was a mean drunk, emotionally and physically violent. He was so angry his face went deep, deep red, like his head might explode. As a young child I thought it just might. The jowls of flesh on his face swung and sweat flew off him. Blue eyes bulged. Teeth pushed forward. He was terrifying.

Mum cowered, covering her body with her arms and crying. She could not get to us, my sister and me, as we were on the other side of the kitchen, a table separating us. He left the room without hurting anyone, but he might as well have. His rage filled the room, filled the house. I did not understand why he raged, just that he did, and he terrified my mother. She was taller than he, but in the moments after he left the room and she came to comfort us she seemed suddenly small, young, and terrifyingly vulnerable.

Sometimes, late at night, the ringing of the phone would wake us up. It would be one of Dad's friends, calling Mum to warn her he was in a bad way and heading home. Mum would pull on her dressing gown and rush us all out of bed and into the car. No time for getting dressed. Time to run, time to hide.

But she never hid very well, for she always went to the same place. Friends who lived nearby would let us in, make us as comfortable as they could in their lounge, and we would wait. Eventually Dad would turn up, furious his family had embarrassed him in this way.

She felt dirty. What a cliché! But that's how she felt. As though she had been initiated into a club she didn't want to belong to, but could not escape. Why she felt this way she was not sure. The old bastard had molested her for years, but he hadn't actually raped her. Why did she feel so bad?

She had forgotten much of the detail of the night, so many years ago, that her deep, deep shame began. The memory of it that had surfaced that night with her first love had been so horrifying she had promptly repressed it back into the vault of her memory. So once again, the details of the rape suppressed, she was left carrying just the feeling, the knowledge it had happened and her intense discomfort.

Often dressing in the black of the gothic culture she felt a little better. She could hide behind the black, people looked at her because of her clothes not her difference, she had hidden it so well. If only she could have known that the only one seeing her difference then was her.

What was so different about her? The way she saw the world, for one thing. She didn't know anyone else who cried at the news. Cried at the images of war, of children being carried away from bomb sites, bloodied and lifeless or wailing inconsolably for parents who would not be coming. Cried at the racist bigotry her parents spoke, the television promoted, could they really not see that their beliefs were cruel and full of hatred? Hatred for what? For people they would never know, whose lives they could not even imagine from the comfort of their lounge chairs.

Why is it so easy for people to hate? Why does it take such little effort to tap into a deep well of ugliness, cruel words, hatred for something they don't even understand?

Why do men with money rule over all with their iron fists and iron hearts? Why does money talk more loudly than animals, nature, the incredible luxury of forests? Do they not hear the sounds of the forest? The movement of the trees, the trilling of birds, little grunts of animals as they move about their day. Are they so deaf and blind they can neither see nor hear the magic of the environment they destroy every day? Do they not care for the lives of the thousands of creatures who live in every acre of forest they tear down?

She is overwhelmed by her need to stop these people. To save the animals, the creatures, the trees, all of it. How? At least on the radio she has a voice. Her listeners come largely from the environmental lobby, so they encourage her, calling her to say hey, we've got a petition going at the moment, can you give that a mention in your show today? A big-name band is coming to town, can you promote that? We're holding a benefit concert to raise money to support the forest angels who protect the forest from the logging machines. Can you let people know and see how much money we can raise to support them?

Slowly, a little bit of her awakened. She still didn't fully remember why she felt so ashamed, so different, but for now she was happy. She had purpose. She was making a difference. She belonged. And just as she began to feel really alive for the first time in a very, very long time, the tarnishing began.

When metal tarnishes it gradually darkens, changes colour, until all its shine is hidden under the tarnish.

That first phone call in the night, enquiring after her underwear, the tarnishing process began. If she could remember she would understand why it rattled her as much as it did, but she couldn't. So she told her friends, told her boyfriend who had returned to her. And she kept talking, kept playing music, and just waited for the sullied feeling to go away.

He rang again, and again, and again. He didn't really have anything to say, he just liked hearing her voice and tormenting her with his inappropriate personal questions. His favourite question was to ask what sort of underwear she was wearing, followed by telling her how sexy her voice was. Did she know she was a tease? Why did she do that, tease him and not come across?

Was she afraid of him? She should be, he would say. She felt afraid of him, even though she didn't know who he was. She got braver and braver, telling him not to call, hanging up the phone, then taking the studio phone off the hook so no one could call. At least if he was a real freak, and she was right to be afraid, she knew the local police station listened to her during the night.

All she had to do was call for help through the microphone.

Chapter 8

෴ Don't Panic ෴

The first time he arrived in the building she was alone in the studio. It was in the early hours of the morning and she felt his presence before he made it known. Logically she knew he could not be in the building, could not have gotten through the security door at the bottom of the stairs. But he had, she could feel it.

She also knew she was a sitting duck. In the studio there was one door in and the same one door was the only way out. The big studio window looked out into the control room, where a large rack of electronic equipment blinked coloured lights constantly.

As the main lights went out and the control room was plunged into darkness, the tiny coloured lights that continued to blink seemed to say run, run! But she couldn't. She was confined to the studio. He stood between her and the one door out.

Quickly she moved to wedge a chair under the handle of the closed studio door. The thickness of the door gave her some relief. Surely he couldn't get through that?

The studio window was huge, almost the width of the wall and about two feet high. But it was toughened glass and a double layer. Designed to be sound proof, she hoped it was also bullet proof.

Now what? He was only a few feet away, disguised by the darkness. He could see her in the brightly lit studio, but she could not see him. She sat down at her desk, put another record on, a long one, and picked up the phone.

"You'll have to come down and open the door," her friend said.

"I can't," she wailed, "he's in here! I have to get past him to open the door."

"What do you want me to do?" he asked.

"Okay, okay," she whispered, "see you in ten minutes."

Terror flooded through her, momentarily making all movement impossible as she waited. And then she was up, pulling the chair away from the door, running across the darkened control room, down the three flights of stairs to the security door at the street. All the while waiting for him to hit her, grab her from behind as she ran. Waiting for the feeling of the promised knife in her back he had threatened, the knife that would take her life.

She opened the door and almost fell weeping into the arms of her friend. But she didn't, she regained her composure.

Finding speech difficult, she managed to point up the stairs.

"He's up there, in the dark. He let himself in. I don't know how." And the friend went up the stairs, seemingly unafraid. She followed, feeling braver in his company. At the top of the stairs they went through the door to the radio station, looked down the hallway and walked into the control room. Lights switched on straight away.

Room by room they searched for him. The toilet, the tiny kitchen, the library, the office, under desks, behind doors.

"He's not here now that's for sure," he announced calmly. She wasn't sure, but she felt braver, more confident. She had called for help and help came. She made coffee, the awful cheap instant coffee that somehow tastes wonderful in the middle of the night when there is nothing else.

Reassuring the friend, yes, she would be okay, she encouraged him to go home, get some sleep.

Finally back in the studio, she propped the chair against the heavy studio door again. Her friend would think her silly, but it made her feel better. Turning on the microphone, she apologised for the record that had finished playing some time ago and was now clicking insistently.

She spoke only a few words into the microphone before stopping abruptly. The lights in the control room went off. She was pitched into darkness again. Him on the dark side of the glass, her on the lit side. She cried, muffled sounds making it into the microphone, past the fingers she had placed firmly against her mouth.

The phones began to ring. Callers concerned for her, wanting to help. She did not need to pick up the calls to know this. It brought her comfort but did not allay her terror.

Moving towards the door, terrified it would slam open, crushing the chair that held it shut and her in its path, she turned off the light.

The studio was lit dimly now by the lights of the console, the phone and the few pieces of equipment. She knew he could still see her, but she felt less laid bare without the glare of the main lights.

Sitting back down, willing herself to keep breathing, don't panic, you'll get through this. The chair will hold the door. She set more music playing and took a few calls, thanking people for their concern, assuring them everything was fine. Just an electrical hitch she said calmly. The lights went out and it gave me a fright.

Some time later she felt him leave. Of course, the sun had begun to rise and light was entering the control room now. He didn't want to be seen. He liked to watch but did not want to be seen.

Turning up the music so loud the speakers shook and the glass windows vibrated, she sang louder than she ever had. She had survived! People she didn't even know cared for her safety. This studio was home to her and she wasn't going to give it up lightly.

The phone calls continued. One night she didn't hang up as fast as usual. His words struck her mute and paralysed her with terror.

"You didn't stay long at your mother's last night," he said. He kept talking but all she heard was, "Your sister, that's your sister isn't it? I like her."

How did he know where she had been? How did he know what her relationship to other people was? Had he been watching her all this time? Too much. This is too much. Am I not safe anywhere?

He often talked about a long-bladed knife he loved to use, how she would not see it coming. The first she would know would be the moment she felt it against her spine, before he plunged it into her. She would know then, in public, on the street, or perhaps in the private space of her bed, that he had claimed her. She could not say no to him then.

"You like going to the bakery, maybe there," he said, then added, "you don't have to make it so hard. I might go for your sister instead. I can gut fish, you know."

From that day she tried not to sleep alone. There was often a male asleep on the couch or in the room next to hers. Friends, her father, her boyfriend, her flatmate. This brought comfort. Until the terrible night Fido disappeared. Fido was about three months old. A pretty, lively kitten coloured black, orange and white (tortoiseshell) with huge green eyes. Fido was one of six kittens she had hand-raised after their mother cat died suddenly. She was hit by a car when they were only one week old. Fido had been missing for a day, which was really out of place, he just didn't wander away from home or her. She didn't let him outside on his own either, so it really made no sense.

A friend had arrived at the door, just as a group were preparing at her home for a night of drinking and dance.

"I'm really sorry," he said, "I think your cat has been hit by a car. He's down by the road." Running down the stairs to the street she saw his little body. As though a brick had slammed into her chest she felt unable to breathe, unable to do anything. A strange sound came from her as she held his body, limp, cool and bloodied. She wanted to hug him back to life, kiss him, love him back to living.

Instead she agreed to bury him in the church yard next door. Someone had a spade in their car, so the process was quick. She sat afterwards looking at the small rise in the dirt and talking to Fido, begging his forgiveness. She didn't know why but she felt it was her fault.

The next night, still hungover from drinking too much the night before after Fido's burial, she was back in the radio studio. Across the road, sleeping in her bed, were Elvis, an incredibly gentle light silver tabby kitten and Sooty, sweet and playful, with a very dark grey, almost black coat. They were Fido's brother and sister. She had been unable to part with the three babies, so kept them as her family. That night she felt sombre as she allowed herself to get into the shift. A little after one a.m. the phone lit up.

"I'm so sorry," he said, "so sorry about little Fido."

The voice drifted off a bit, giving her time to wonder in fear how he knew Fido's name, or what had happened to Fido?

The voice continued talking.

"Fido, he cried a lot," he said. "Every time his head smashed into the wall, he cried. He cried for you. You didn't come. You should have. I did it for you. There were too many people around, I couldn't get to you."

"Oh God, no!" she screamed as she disconnected the phone. She could see Fido, his beautiful little body being swung repeatedly into the brick wall, his cries of pain, his cries for help. Her heart felt like it would explode. She left the studio, ran home, locked herself in her flat with her two remaining babies and cried. She cried, long, hard, gut-wrenching sobs that left her exhausted yet awake, terrified to drop her guard lest he come back.

Even as these words make their way onto the page, many years later, she fights them. She still screams, "No! No! No! Please no."

But it was true. In the morning, after a dark night of grief and terror, she began to question how it was that Fido came to be outside. She kept the flat well-locked, even when she was at home, to keep the owner of the voice out. How had he gotten in? He must have gotten in somehow to get Fido and take him outside to his death?

And she remembered. Little Bear, tiny Little Bear. A small black and white kitten, only months old when he disappeared. She hadn't told anyone about that, and yet the Stalker had offered his commiserations. How had he known? Oh no, that's just too much to take in.

Now what? How could she keep Elvis and Sooty safe? Their dear little faces smiled as they slept, tearing at her heart.

Chapter 9

∽ **Nowhere to Run** ∽

She tried to share her fear, but the first person she told responded quickly.

"You're just emotional, it is sad, but you know Fido just got hit by a car. It happens all the time."

The second person responded similarly, then the next, and the next. Why wouldn't anyone believe her?

She felt she had to leave, go away, disappear for a while. From her island home of Tasmania, she took the overnight boat to Melbourne, on Mainland Australia. Two friends went too. They were hoping to get work, stay a few months and earn enough to pay a few bills before coming home. Elvis and Sooty went to stay with her sister. She knew how much her sister loved animals, so felt they would be safe with her.

One month into the Melbourne adventure, Elvis and Sooty disappeared.

"How?" she cried, "how is that possible? Did you keep them inside? Did you feed them?"

"I haven't been home much, they may have gone a day or so without food. Maybe they got hungry and went looking?" the sister replied.

Oh good God, she thought, they are gone and it is my fault. I really am alone in this. Her sister was not to blame. She was young too, twenty-one at the time, and had also suffered great trauma. Only eighteen months older, so many times she had played a mothering role to the wide-eyed girl, buying her clothes, providing her with cash and food when it was needed. The responsibility she had shouldered for her younger siblings in situations they had all been far too young to fully understand had been an unfair and terrible burden.

The wide-eyed girl was in no rush to go home now. There were no cats to worry about or care for. She stayed in Melbourne another month or so before returning to her beloved radio station. The little flat was quiet now. No meows in the night, no gentle purr under her chin as she slept. All three babies were gone. And she believed it was her fault, she had failed them all.

At least she still had the radio. She was promoted, weekday breakfast-show host! The golden girl, some called her. This was the pinnacle of radio, being offered the breakfast show! It was public radio, there was no pay, no reward, but she loved it. She even got good at getting out of bed bright and early to get there. Living across the road helped!

With the cats gone there was little for him to take from her now. What more could he do? Then a new kitten arrived. Her mother's friend had thought it might help. But this one she did not speak of on the radio. She kept this little one private. Ocelot, she called her. A sweet, playful kitten, she had the softest coat. Light grey, white and a very light ginger.

Then she woke one morning, looked around her small room and realised her clothing had been removed from the hanging rack and placed on the floor. Shoes had moved from one side of the room to the other. Only she and her flatmate had been home all night, she was sure of it. Running to the main entrance door (the only entrance to the apartment) she checked, yes it was locked. The windows were locked. How had he done it?

She got confirmation it was him on her next early morning shift at the radio when he called.

"How did you like your clothes?" he asked, "your shoes were a bit messy."

She felt sick. Although she knew it had been him, she had clung to the hope that it was her flatmate or boyfriend having a laugh. Hanging up the phone she continued her show, feeling disjointed, as though she might leave her body at any moment and just float away over the city.

This was to be the first of many late-night visits. No matter what she did he always found a way in. She would wake up to find things moved around in the kitchen, shoes lined up in unusual ways around the house.

Dad and the wide-eyed girl hadn't been too close in recent years, but he was pretty keen on catching the mongrel who was stalking his daughter.

"Don't worry," he said proudly, "I'll stay on the lounge. Bastard won't get past me." Bastard did! Dear old Dad was asleep on the couch, snoring so loudly the Stalker could have bashed saucepans together as he went past and not woken him.

And yet, as the Stalker let himself back out the large lounge-room window, a window that led out onto the awning of the store below, Dad finally woke up. He bellowed an almighty roar and charged, trying to grab him in a rugby tackle. Had Dad woken a second or two earlier this might have done the job. But the Stalker was just far enough away and just quick enough to avoid Dad's grasp. As she entered the room she saw the Stalker hoisting himself head first out the window, heading for the awning, her father holding desperately onto his trouser leg.

Dad swore profusely as the Stalker disappeared over the awning. She cried. Dad swore some more. They were so close to catching him! The boyfriend appeared from the laneway below.

"I've got his car licence plate!" he cried, "we've got the bastard now. Let's get this traced and pay him a visit! Give him a bit of his own medicine!"

It never happened, and she was grateful. She was afraid of what he and his mates might do, they might go too far and get themselves into terrible trouble. Their drunken promises of action had been pretty final.

In her mind's eye she could see them hurling his lifeless body into the boot of a car. The thought of any of them going to prison for defending her was a huge responsibility she was not willing to entertain.

She did report the incident and the details of his car, the make and model, colour and licence plates to the police. But yet again, as no crime appeared to have been committed, nothing was done. The officers she spoke to expressed concern and compassion, but the law as it stood at the time prevented any action being taken.

It was quiet for a little while after that. She began to feel normal. There was radio, dancing on the weekend, a busy social life. Then one evening noises on the roof called her attention. She listened for some time, before heading outside to look up onto the roof. Seeing nothing, she began to move down the steps towards the street below, when he called out her name.

She froze at first, not sure what to do. Turning towards the voice she saw his silhouette. He was standing on the roof of her neighbour's apartment, and he was holding a small gun which he aimed squarely at her. She moved down the steps as fast as she could, when he called her name again.

On the driveway now, back to the brick wall where Fido had taken his last breath, she stood and stared at him.

He laughed. Then he fired the shot. One solitary shot.

The bullet landed in the wall to her left. Something inside her snapped and she was off, running for her life. Over the road, fumbling with the lock on the security door to the radio station. In the building and up the stairs she ran as fast as she could. Barging into the studio she begged the surprised announcer to call the police. Then she changed her mind. Instead, she went to them.

A female officer at the police station explained there was nothing she could do.

"This is crazy," the wide-eyed girl cried. "We gave you his licence plates. We gave you the colour and model of his car. Surely you can use that to find out who he is? What more do you want?"

"There's nothing we can do," said the officer, "there is no proof. So far he has threatened rather than actually hurt you."

"Threatened? What about my cat? What are you going to do about him?" she screamed.

"There's still nothing we can do. If he hurts you, actually assaults you, then we can do something."

She swore then, terrified and frustrated. The closest the police ever came to laying charges in this mess was that night, as the officer threatened to charge her for swearing at a police officer.

"Surely," she asked, "you have the record of all the times I've called, all the things he has done? It's been going on a long time!"

"There aren't any records," the policewoman bravely explained, "as there haven't been any assaults, nothing we can charge him with."

"You can't charge him with stalking me? Killing my cat – we know he did that, he called me to boast! Shooting at me? If you look the bullet will be in the wall."

"I'm sorry," replied the officer, "but the way the law stands we can't do anything unless he actually hurts you."

Chapter 10

✎ New Beginnings ✎

Again, she felt alone, even with the support of the men in her life. What was the point of the police if they only ever turned up after the fact and would not, or could not, do anything to prevent him coming back and having another go?

She knew they did their best, but felt like the police didn't believe her. Her family, apart from Dad, certainly didn't.

"You've just got a ridiculous imagination," Mum said, repeatedly, "why would anyone bother to chase you? What makes you think you're that interesting? You're nothing special."

Ocelot disappeared. He didn't call to boast, so there was hope she might return. The area outside her apartment had been enclosed with a huge fishing net for Elvis and Sooty months earlier. Ocelot had been allowed to play out here, for the girl had become braver. And he didn't know about Ocelot, she was only allowed out when the girl was there. But she disappeared anyway. When he called, weeks had passed.

"It's a shame about your pretty cat," he said slowly, "she would have been lovely for her fur. The other two, you miss them?"

She was barely breathing, afraid of what he might say next. She wanted more than anything to hang up the phone, but she waited.

"Can you see their little bodies?" he asked. She could. As he described the knife he had used, spearing each small cat through the chest and anchoring them to a door, she could see it. Every horrible detail.

Where? Whose door? Why? She felt their cries, fear, despair. Her beautiful, beautiful babies. She remembered how wonderful it had felt to hold them as babies, their tiny warm bodies in her hand, comforting them as she fed them special formula from a bottle. Their dear little faces, dark eyes, and the lovely noises they had made as they suckled. She remembered them growing larger, beautiful shiny coats, big voices and rumbling purrs.

All just a memory now. She hadn't been there to protect them when they needed her. This time she didn't tell a soul. She couldn't bear hearing the apparently reasonable explanations that might be offered, or that there was nothing that could be done.

"You need to lock your doors, secure your windows. He knows where you are," she explained to her family.

"You're paranoid," they said.

No one took her seriously, or considered themselves at risk. Her sister in particular refused to take any precautions to keep herself safe from him. She made a point of leaving doors and windows unlocked and open. She wasn't going to live in fear.

This was terrifying to the wide-eyed girl, as the Stalker often made comments about her sister, how easy it was to watch her. As if to make sure she believed he had, he would describe in intimate detail the contents of her kitchen, the layout of her house, what she had cooked for dinner or who she had been out drinking with.

Rapunzel, the curious analogy of the woman who lives in a turret, protected from the input and energy of anybody else. And yet, eventually, she is tempted by one who is called to awaken her interest and she is able to finally find the courage and the way to leave her turret and take part in life again.

The turret is the fear. You have been so afraid of harm coming to your animals. So afraid of another lunatic coming along and hurting them.

And yet you have had the courage to leave them at home and go out in the world, searching, looking for your key.

Do not judge yourself or punish yourself for your fears, they have pushed you along in the direction you have needed to go. There's blessed irony!

She wanted to be defiant, to be rebellious and leave doors open, to believe as her sister did that all was well with the world and there was no reason to be afraid. In the end she moved in with her sister, into a share house made up of two apartments and housing six people. Safety in numbers! And it was fun for a while to have so much company.

Then something fabulous happened. She had been encouraged by her peers to audition for the commercial radio training course run in Sydney by the Australian Film, Television and Radio School. Just the thought of it took her breath away. Swallowing the butterflies that danced vigorously in her stomach, she applied.

"I don't know why you're bothering," Mum said. "I can't imagine what you think makes you so special. They won't look at you."

"She will do well," said Nanna, before reaching over to take the wide-eyed girl's hand in her own warm, wrinkled hand, "don't listen to your mother."

Nanna was right. She was offered an audition! They would fly her to Sydney and meet her at the school! Mum, after all she had said, cried with joy and took her shopping, paying for a suitable outfit for the big event. She hadn't been to Sydney since she was a child. She went, spent a day with her grandparents there, and gave the interview her best.

They chose her! She couldn't believe it!

In a matter of weeks, she had moved into a little house, situated in the middle of a carpark, on the campus of Macquarie University, North Ryde. She shared this house with the other students. Amazed that she was there, she was nervous but incredibly excited. Her fellow students, eleven other equally keen radio buffs, were people she liked. She truly couldn't believe her luck!

Over the space of three months they learned how to produce a radio program, write news articles and commercial copy. They played endlessly in the professional studios, learning how to mix music, how to present. What she really enjoyed was the voice coaching with the Marlboro Man, Arch McKirdy. Arch had an incredible voice and he sure knew how to use it. She loved hearing him teach, the varying tones and depth to his voice. They called him the Marlboro Man because he had, some years back, voiced the commercials shown in the cinemas around Australia for Marlboro cigarettes. Ads showing the great Australian outback, and Arch's beautifully delivered words, "This… is Marlboro country."

For those months she was not afraid. She didn't watch her back. Engrossed in her studies and practice, the wide-eyed girl thrived. Before she knew it, the course was complete. She had graduated Highly Commended and felt a great sense of achievement. What would happen now? Would she be offered a job? Was she skilled enough?

She didn't really believe she was good enough, but she went home to Hobart and waited. A few short weeks later and the school phoned. We have a job for you, they said, at a radio station in country New South Wales. Lismore. A lovely town built on a flood plain.

Chapter 11

 Bad Dreams

1990

Just after her 21st birthday and Christmas celebrations, she and the boyfriend packed everything into a car and drove to the boat that would take them over the water to mainland Australia, beginning the journey to Lismore.

Grover, a beautiful silver tabby cat who had arrived as a stray and stayed, and her young kitten, were to be cared for by friends until she had found a home. This might take a few weeks, being a small town. To her dismay Grover didn't hang around. The friends had grown tired of Grover and her baby within days, so delivered her to the wide-eyed girl's mother to care for. However, Grover had fended for herself before and soon found herself a new home.

Driving to Lismore was not the fun adventure she had imagined. Travelling on the ferry over the Bass Strait she was overcome with pain in her jaw. It was almost impossible to talk and she certainly could not eat. Arriving in the port of Melbourne they drove to her aunt's house. Thankfully her aunt knew what to do. Before she could refuse, the wide-eyed girl was in a dentist's chair having x-rays taken. The dentist explained there was no damage, her jaw was shut because the muscles had frozen. A condition called temporomandibular dysfunction and most likely her body's response to stress, and to continually biting down on her truth, not feeling she could speak up.

Still unable to talk, she left Melbourne with a migraine headache and a prescription for mighty strong muscle relaxants. It turned out the tablets were a bit of a blessing. The boyfriend's car didn't travel well in the heat of the Melbourne summer, even less once they crossed the border to New South Wales. The air conditioner failed and the car just kept getting hotter and hotter. She was grateful for the tablets that relieved the pain and made her drowsy.

During the drive they stopped at the Bathurst car racing track. How excited the boyfriend was to drive a lap. Both imagined the track as they had seen it on television on race days. Speed, flags, fast voices, fast cars, and lots of people cheering on the drivers. They stayed in country hotels, some of the most uncomfortable beds she would ever sleep in. And still her mouth remained mainly shut.

Her arrival at the radio station in Lismore, dishevelled from the hot drive, barely able to talk, was not how she had imagined it! She was unable to make herself understood as clearly as she would have liked, as her jaw was almost but not entirely healed. She had been forced to lean close to the receptionist and speak slowly, with great intent, to explain who she was and why she was there.

The receptionist, a short, dark haired woman with generous, dancing eyes, made a call and before long a tall, not-too-pleased looking man appeared. She was so mortified by her inability to speak clearly, she didn't remember much of the greeting. Lucky I can write commercials as well as talk, she thought, a moment before the man said as much.

She stayed a year in that job. Writing commercials, doing live shifts on air, writing environmental alerts, dreaming about working her way into the news room, that looked exciting! But it wasn't to be. None of that year was what she imagined. Before she had even settled in, life changed dramatically.

It was the day before Valentine's Day. It had started out a normal day, but during the night she awoke from the most awful nightmare, crying and inconsolable. She had seen her Nanna, sitting in her armchair, but she was dead. Gone. Just like that.

"It's just a dream," the boyfriend encouraged as he held her, "just a dream."

The next day, early afternoon, the call came.

"It's Mum," the tearful voice quivered, then all she heard was crying. She knew. Her sister's voice came through the phone, "It's Nanna," she wavered, "she's gone."

Knees crumbled, she missed the chair and landed on the floor in disbelief. The phone in her hand still, but not to her ear, she heard her sister say something about Nanna going to sleep in her favourite chair and not waking up. "Must have been a heart attack," was the last thing she remembered hearing.

A colleague drove her home. She was vaguely aware of making phone calls, organising a loan from her other grandmother to pay for airfares to travel home immediately for the funeral. Enduring a lecture from her grandmother on the ills of borrowing money, and her demands that she take the debt seriously and begin paying her back on her very next pay packet, she wondered how her grandmothers could be so different.

Then she was alone in her grief. Nanna would have asked how she was, is someone there with her, is she okay? Alone in the flat above the pub, it was hard to breathe, her head hurt fit to explode. A knock on the door pulled her out of her stupor briefly. Opening the door, she stared at the boyfriend.

"Shit," he said, "you look like someone's died!"

She collapsed. The most important person in her world was gone. Nanna was the one she went to, bared her soul to. Nanna just got her, understood her. Telling him made it real.

In the daze that only great shock can bring, the next morning she suffered what seemed like a never-ending drive to the airport. An hour or so away, that's all, the boyfriend had encouraged. And then she was there, in her mother's house, surrounded by faces that told her it was not a dream. Her nightmare had become reality.

The phone rang. It was Mum's younger sister. Did anyone want to view Nanna's body in the morning? Yes! She did. The thought of it terrified her but she wanted so badly to say goodbye.

"No!" Mum shrieked, "you can't, how could you? That's disgusting! You can't leave me here alone!"

Thus, she never did say goodbye directly. At the funeral the next morning she lingered outside, not able to walk into the funeral parlour. This is not how she wanted things to be. This is not the kind of place she could have imagined seeing off Nanna. When she thought of Nanna she saw her gardens, the roses and flowers she tended with great care, colour and life everywhere. This place was a red brick box, little to no garden, concrete out front. Stark, lacking life and colour, this was not Nanna.

Looking up to the sky she was surprised to hear a long, loud wail. She did not recognise her own voice as it tore through her like a knife, opening the wound of grief so wide she could drown in it.

Arms were around her. A familiar voice, her aunt, encouraging her to come inside. Her aunt, her own features wracked with grief, understood her pain. Guiding her inside, she sat beside her and the service began.

Whoever was leading the service hadn't done his homework. He didn't get Nanna's name right. She wanted to jump up, scream at him for the disrespect he had shown. She didn't. She sat. Did she want to go to the crematorium for the short service before burning of the body? She went, not wanting to let go of Nanna one moment before she absolutely had to. Her father, brother and sister stood beside her.

The chapel was small, and up front and centre was Nanna's coffin. The process was swift. The coffin began to disappear and before she could comprehend the finality, Nanna was gone. Outside once more, trying to breathe the fresh air, she smelt the smoke. Was it Nanna burning? Probably not, but at the time she thought it was. She would forever remember this day, the smell, and her horror.

Chapter 12

∽ **Goodbye** ∽

So many people at the morning tea at her uncle's that followed. Hard to cope. An old woman, who looked so much like her Nanna it was hard to look her in the eye, sat next to the wide-eyed girl. Her eyes were not so much wide now as weeping, swollen and very red. Listening to the old woman speak was creating a sense of panic in her, the similarity to Nanna too much to bear. She's an aunt I suppose. Mum told her later they were cousins of some sort.

Apologising as she made her exit, she left the gathering to wander across the property to Nanna's house. Nanna had lived for many years on the same property as her eldest son, so it was not far to walk.

Entering through the side door, she slowly wandered into the convict-built cottage, which was gently warmed by the sun. The smell of Nanna's cooking still hung in the air. The kitchen to the right looked and felt as it always had. She let her hand sweep slowly across the bench, to the warm airing cupboard where she and Nanna had raised so many sickly ducklings.

She smiled, remembering the year the duck population had swelled to more than fifty. Only young at the time, she had let them into Nanna's sunroom, for a tea party. In a flash of remembrance, she could hear Nanna's scream, the click of her false teeth as she clapped her hands and stamped her foot furiously, ushering the ducks back outside.

As punishment, she had told the wide-eyed-girl to clean every last bit of duck pooh from the sunroom. It took her a few hours. Unluckily for her, she had not collected the Legos that were strewn across the floor before she let the ducks in. Soaking and scrubbing the pooh from the hundreds of pieces of Lego took a very long time. She remembered how angry Nanna had been, but also how the corners of Nanna's mouth had crept up into a smile when she thought the girl was not looking.

Eyes glancing to the table, she allowed herself to imagine Nanna pouring a cup of tea from her old tea pot. A small laugh escaped as she noticed the latest knitted teapot cosy adorning Nanna's favourite pot! This beautiful woman, the woman who had always defended her, who taught her to paint, draw, sew, raise orphaned ducklings – was gone. As much as the house still smelt and felt of her, she was gone. Undeniable.

Wandering through the rest of the house she remembered the day her father had come for her. She had been only twelve or thirteen then. Dad had moved out some months earlier. Mum was still struggling to look after the kids and had sent her wide-eyed girl to live with Nanna.

"I'm taking her," Dad had said to Nanna. Nanna had come out of her cottage and cocked her head sideways, looking at Dad as though she was considering what he had to say.

"Are you now?" Nanna had enquired. "Where to?"

"She needs care, I'm taking her to foster care," Dad said, not sounding too convincing.

Wide-eyed girl caught her breath in fear. She had heard enough about foster care to know she never wanted to go there! Nanna, gentle, funny, loving Nanna, reared up like a dragon and spoke with a volume and firmness she had never before witnessed.

"You are NOT taking my granddaughter anywhere! She is safe and happy here, with me, and she is staying. Get off my property!"

And he did. Dad had made his grand gesture, his feeble attempt at parenting. Turning without a word, he got back in his old heap of a car and drove off. Neither said anything for what seemed like an eternity as they watched the car make its way down the drive and out onto the road.

Then Nanna pulled her close, held her tight, and cried, all the while voicing some pretty strong words against Dad. Who did he think he was to march in here after being absent for months? Following Nanna back into the house, she heard her own voice jabbering away about her father's cheek to turn up thinking to take her away, while Nanna made the inevitable pot of tea.

But inside she had been filled with an odd mixture of emotions. Cold dread at the knowledge that her parents could do such a thing, at any time, warmed to a slightly more hopeful state by the memory of Nanna's fierce defence. As much as she loved living with Nanna, she now knew that she was not safe, not ever. What if he came back, or Mum with some equally hair-brained scheme, and Nanna was not here to defend her? Nothing Nanna could do would warm the chill of dread that now settled into her bones.

Waves of remembrance kept coming, memories unbidden. She sat for a while in the lounge, in a favourite chair. Remembered Friday evenings with Nanna and the old bastard, watching the Two Ronnies on the television. The wood heater crackling quietly, Nanna's false teeth occasionally clicking on the peppermints she chewed and the rhythmic click-clacking of knitting needles. The giraffe flies into memory. The hilarious orange and black giraffe Nanna had knitted for one of her aunt's babies. It was super cute, but had a very long neck so the head always collapsed on the floor.

Time to go. She can hear footsteps crunching on the hard pavers outside. She knows she will never step into this space, Nanna's space, again. The ache sets in and she makes herself leave. Back to the small talk, back to people who don't really know her, back to pretending.

Alone. She feels alone the next day as she flies back to Lismore, back to her new job. Back to the boyfriend. She loves him. She seeks security, wanting to know she is safe. But he is a player, loves to go out, like a magnificent ginger cat with his mane of red hair he loves to be stroked, his ego well-fed. She understands this, although she does not like it, she accepts it. He loves her, that she is sure of. Better than being alone. She was terrified of that. So many nights she had been alone and the Stalker had terrorised her, taken from her.

Weeks later her grief had not eased. She was doing what was expected of her, going to work, writing commercials at a fast pace, presenting on air as often as she could. But her heart was broken, shattered into fragments she could not recognise.

One evening, just at dusk, she was in the live studio, microphone on, when a colleague stepped silently into the studio, a cardboard box in her hands. Smiling, she pointed at the wide-eyed girl, placed her hands on her heart, then turned and left.

Through her headphones, the girl heard the faintest little squeak. Her heart leapt in her chest! She knew that sound! Microphone off, music playing, she darted around the desk to open the box. Small, fluffy, silver tabby.

"Sam!" she exclaimed, naming the tiny kitten in a flash as she took him into her arms and held him close to her chest. Tears flowed, hot and fast, as the life in her arms stirred, waved a little paw at her and let out another squeak.

Sam grew fast, so fast that people began to ask her if he might be a Maine Coone. Probably, she would say with pride, but really, he's just a farm cat. Eventually he grew so big she almost believed he was a Maine Coone! Sam worked his magic, helping her heal. The year at Lismore wasn't easy, but it was not as lonely now. The boyfriend worked a lot, so they didn't spend as much time together as she might have liked. But she still felt so sad, it was hard for her to imagine anyone would actually want to be around her. Sometimes she thought about counselling, for she knew her grief was not abating, but she was terrified of being labelled insane.

Years ago, before she was ten, she had spoken freely of her feelings, of all that she could see and hear that others couldn't. The fairies in the backyard, the people who came to talk to her. Invisible to everyone else, but not to her. Frightened by this, her parents had driven her to the prison nearby.

"This is where you will end up, if you don't stop telling stories about imaginary friends," they said. This terrified her, but didn't stop her.

Another Sunday drive, this time to the Psychiatric Hospital.

"If you don't go to prison, you will end up here," they said, "and we won't be allowed in to visit you here."

That did it. No more talking about anything that might seem out of the ordinary. As a young girl, when she had been far too young to understand, she had seen actor Jack Nicholson's character tragically monstered in the film "One Flew Over the Cuckoo's Nest."

Having also experienced her mother's prolonged nervous breakdown, and witnessed so many times her mother's fear of being labelled insane and being locked in a psychiatric ward, she was never going to ask for help. Becoming her mother just didn't bear thinking about, so she just kept on going. Until she couldn't.

Chapter 13

∽ Homeward ∾

Home, she had to go home. Never mind the career, she needed family around her. A year free of the Stalker's harassment, she had forgotten what it felt like to be afraid. Forgotten how scary it was to walk down the street, knowing her life might be taken at any moment. Home to Hobart. No job and no boyfriend, for he stayed in Lismore for a while.

From the highs of radio school and a paid job, she went to a country town to work as a barmaid and waitress. At first it was fun for her, a relief from the pressure of writing commercials. Away from the competition she had not handled well of the other junior staff at the radio station. Boarding with the chef and his wife, she and Sam were safe, cared for.

She could have stayed, enjoyed the work, the security. If only she hadn't begun the affair. Before the affair, she had been dating an old friend. Sadly, his ability to express emotion was almost as challenged as hers, so it was brief and ended badly. She felt they had a relationship, but was confused by his apparent lack of commitment. Naïve, she still had very little understanding of how to be in a relationship, or of her own worth. Thus when the next man came along, said he had to be with her, would love her forever, leave his wife, she believed him. Of course he did no such thing, instead left her alone and pregnant.

Pregnant! She was so excited!

"Don't be ridiculous," Mum said, "you can't raise a baby! Don't expect him to support you! You'll be on your own!"

And she was, for eventually she had lied and told him she didn't love him. She had come back down to earth and didn't feel she had the right to demand anything of him. His wife already had a child, she needed him more. Smiling as she felt her belly, she knew she would love this baby enough for them both.

For the first time in her life she wasn't afraid to live on her own. She was working in radio again now, only as the girl driving around Hobart giving away freebies on the breakfast show, but she loved it! Sometimes she wrote commercials, and she was given shifts on the evenings and weekends. Her dream come true! A paid gig on commercial radio in Hobart!

Just as everything seemed perfect it all came crashing down. She lost the baby. Who loses a baby, she asks? Makes it sound like she went shopping and left her in the supermarket trolley, never to be seen again! The baby miscarried only weeks into the pregnancy.

Alone, she had woken up in the night with sharp pains in her abdomen. She made her way downstairs, out the back door and into the outhouse. The house she rented had been built in the 1800s, with the bathroom and toilet housed in a small wooden outbuilding in the backyard. Sitting on this toilet in the dark of the night she felt intense grief as the baby she felt sure was a girl left her body. The bloody mass that went down the toilet gave no indication, but she knew. Madeline would have been her name.

What would she have given for a loving pair of arms to hold her now, a soothing voice to reassure her she would be okay. She ached for companionship in that moment. How lonely she felt grieving her baby silently in the dark.

"Don't be ridiculous," said Mum the next day, "you can't have had a miscarriage. You do tell stories!"

"You'll be fine," said the old doctor as he patted her hand in what he thought was a soothing manner, "nothing to be done."

Her best friend didn't understand her loss either.

"You dodged a bullet there, what would you do with a baby?" her girlfriend had asked, taking another drag of her third cigarette during her short visit and holding her coffee cup out in front of her for a refill.

She would have loved the baby, that's what she would have done! In the short time she was pregnant she had spent a good deal of time imagining life with her child, how they would be together.

Unlike her bullet-dodging friend, she was not afraid of welcoming a baby into her life. To her this new life was so very precious. And in a heartbeat there was no new life. Dreams shattered, baby gone as though she never existed. There was no one to comfort her, and so hushed, shamed into silence, she carried her loss alone. She could not have known she had just lost the only child her body would ever carry.

Chapter 14

∽ Past into Present ∽

Her grief transmuted into creativity. She began making hand-painted underwear. It sold well! Little red daisies on a white stretch cotton lycra. It seemed she made good shirts too, and before long she was designing and selling them at the local market and in a boutique store. Living alone, except for Sam, the cat she had been given after her Nanna's death, and a beautiful little red heeler cross dog, Zoe Devon, she was happy!

Moving into the little terrace house on her own had terrified her at first. The bedroom was upstairs, up a rickety old open slat staircase. What if the Stalker came here? How would she get out? She would be a sitting duck.

But something in her made her do it. She didn't want her life to be dictated by him, by her fear of him and what he might do. Besides, she was free of him now. She had been away long enough for him to forget. Now it was up to her to be brave, forget and get on with her life.

The on-air studio at the radio station faced onto the parking area, with a fully glassed wall and glass entrance doors, which provided no privacy at all. There was absolutely nowhere to hide.

She first became aware of car headlights shining in at her one evening. Oh good, she thought, someone's come to visit. But no one got out of the car, it just sat there, lights staring at her.

Fear started to grow inside her, tightening her throat, her chest, knotting in her gut. Waiting for a song to start, she walked out of the studio, toward the glass doors. The car slowly backed away, lights still on, then straightened up and drove off.

In a moment all the fear, the terror of life before Lismore came flooding back. Weeping so hard she fought for breath, she told herself no! It can't be him, not again.

She left the station that night on full alert. Every noise in the city street around her amplified. Every smell stronger than usual. Fumbling to unlock her car, she wished it had central locking! Expecting him to ambush her at any moment, she dived into the car, slamming the door and locking it as fast as her terrified fingers would allow. All the while, she kept telling herself to calm down, don't imagine things, it was just someone looking for a park.

A week later she was on air late at night, enjoying the music, feeling how lucky she was to be here in this studio. Turning the speakers down to answer the phone, she answered the call brightly.

"I heard you last week, do you know I thought I saw you last week. But you didn't tell me you were coming home. I thought I was wrong. But I know that voice." And she knew his voice. Slamming the phone down, turning it off at the studio panel so no more calls could come through, she began to shake.

The shaking took over her entire body, slowly, but with such strength she could do nothing but sit. The boss wouldn't be happy, but she managed to hit the repeat button on the song playing. It was all she could do with hands that shook so badly. Tears, silent and wet, fell down her face. Looking out into the street she wished the glass walls were solid, solid brick.

"Please, not again! Please!" she silently begged.

And so began the midnight ritual. Set everything in the studio for overnight, then by 12:30 a.m. she was ready to make the dash, all of about ten metres, from the glass entrance door to her car. She thought about leaving her car unlocked, so she wouldn't have to fumble for the keys. But then what would she do if he hid in the car? She would be trapped in there with him. What if he had the knife he used to threaten her with? She could see herself sitting in the driver's seat, eyes wide open, blood rushing from the wound in her neck. No, she would risk fumbling with the keys.

He kept calling. Did she still have the sexy underwear he used to like?

"I still have the ones I took from you," he boasted. She hung up on him, every time. But she wasn't sure, was it best to hang up and take the phone off the hook, or did that anger him? Would it be better to let him talk, let him feel heard?

He described her sister's house. Asked the wide-eyed girl why she brought the brand of peanut butter she did last Wednesday. Did her mother always cook roast on a Sunday?

He would call, make little statements that let her know he was watching, and then she would hang up the phone.

Sometimes as she drove home he would follow her. Just to make sure she knew it was him, he would boast later. He had this way of following her with his car headlights turned off at first, then turning them on and flashing them on high beam. It was no fun terrorising her if she didn't know.

She learned to drive fast, to take corners so fast she thought she would crash, in her efforts to get away from him. It was enough he could see her and terrorise her at work, damned if she was going to let him find where she lived.

She would drive, get a corner ahead, then pull into a drive, turning her lights off. Her car might be old and didn't have central locking, but it was small and could fit into small spaces. Being dark blue it was also easy to hide at night.

Eventually she asked for help. She tried to explain herself to the station manager, but was afraid of how he might react, afraid he might think her mad and it would cost her the job she enjoyed so much. Had her upbringing not taught her to fear being labelled insane or punished for her claims, she might have presented a better case. Having been doubted, tormented and labelled a story teller for so long, she had many moments when she doubted herself.

"A trace can be put on the studio phone," he said. "Yes," she agreed heartily, that would be good. He also reminded her of the number for the police radio room. She hadn't called them, they had not been able to help in the past.

He continued to torment her, threaten her by stalking her and describing where she had been the day before. He would tell her who she had visited and remind her that she would never know when he was ready to take her life.

But he didn't physically do anything that the police could take action on.

She didn't even know his name and had long ago lost the details of his car registration, so could not provide a solid identification. Apart from being afraid, she felt ashamed. She had brought this on the station and it embarrassed her. Her independence, her power was gone once more.

Chapter 15

 Steak, Sweat and Drugs

The trace on the phone never happened, as it wasn't long after that she lost her job. Media is a cruel industry. You are only as good as your next show, her friend had said to her. So true! In order to pinch another female announcer from the competition radio station down the road, her manager had offered the other announcer her position.

She should have made audition tapes, sent them out across the country. The film and television school would have helped, it may only have been a matter of a few weeks before she could fly to another job somewhere in Australia.

But she couldn't. Frozen by fear, she didn't believe she was good enough anymore. Perhaps she had been kidding herself the whole time. Who was she to think she could have a career in media? And if another station did want her, dare she risk paying the price of attracting stalkers for the rest of her life?

She was still on staff and had agreed to do casual shifts, but she hoped that the irregularity of her shifts would make it hard for him to catch her on air. What was she supposed to do with the rest of her life? She didn't want to do anything but work in radio, nor did she have the skills for another career.

"Fashion school," her sister said, "you love that."

Okay, why not? Nanna had taught her how to sew, she loved it and was good at it. She had made patterns for toys and for her own clothing since she could remember. Her underwear and shirt designs had sold well. She laughed remembering her ten-year-old self and how angry

Mum had been the day she lay down on a new bed sheet, drew around her body, and cut the sheet up to make a pattern for trousers!

Over the next year she went to school, worked part time on the radio whenever shifts were available, and drove like a lunatic to get away from him whenever he tried to follow her. The radio shifts were few and far between in the end, but she didn't do anything to change that.

As the year ended she made plans, with a friend she had made at fashion school, to move to Melbourne. It would be like moving to Lismore, no one would know her, she could be anonymous. He would never find her there, surely? She had long since stopped telling anyone about his attention, his threats. No one seemed to believe her, the police couldn't help her, there was no point. Time to go.

Her father understood, for he had seen and experienced the terror and knew it to be true. Mum wasn't as understanding.

"What's in Melbourne? Why aren't we good enough for you?" she had demanded. By the time she left she had traded in the little blue car for a vintage car, a bright orange 1953 Fiat 1100. Everything she owned piled high, she drove to the other end of Tasmania and caught the boat to Melbourne, mainland Australia.

Her sister had accompanied her, perched beside her on the passenger seat, a suitcase uncomfortably wedged on her lap. Emotions ran high, so hard to say goodbye once more. Perhaps, as the boat pulled out of the harbour at Devonport and her tears fell, she would have felt lighter if she could have seen the ridiculous drive home her sister faced.

The boyfriend had driven with her, in his own little car, so that he might say goodbye and give her sister a lift home. His little car did not fare well, breaking down and overheating, requiring a good deal of attention during the drive home to Hobart. It was an old car that had long since passed its used-by date. The collapsed driver's seat was held in place by a solid plastic milk crate wedged between it and the back seat.

A room in a share house, that would suit her budget and help her meet people. She spent the first few weeks with her aunt and family, at their home and at their holiday home on Phillip Island. It always felt good to spend some time with them, she had enjoyed a strong connection with her aunt for as long as she could remember, and she loved her young cousins.

Her aunt was Nanna's youngest child, eight years younger than Mum. As much as the wide-eyed girl adored her, Mum had always felt jealous. Imagine Mum, socially, physically and emotionally awkward, comparing herself to the younger sister, who of course was as coordinated, capable and physically stunning as Mum believed herself not to be.

Many years later, Mum eventually made peace with her sister, confessing her love for her from her deathbed. The contrast between them had never been more obvious. Aunt, glamourous as always. Mum shrivelled, choking, eyes watering as she struggled to speak and be understood. The power of their last connection was something the wide-eyed girl would never forget.

She found a room in a house near the college she would be attending, so close she could walk to class. Talk about convenient! She moved her meagre belongings in, and agreed to go to the supermarket with her new housemates. The man who held the lease on the property wasn't pretty. Overweight, short of breath, sweating profusely. The other housemate, who moved in the same day as she, worked in a graveyard! She was intrigued. Her fear of death was overridden by curiosity. This man seemed very likeable. He had a good sense of humour, a little bit sharp at times, she would have to watch what she said.

The unlikely trio walked along the busy highway to the supermarket.

"Steak for dinner?" the sweaty one asked. The others agreed in unison. To her horror, he picked up a tray of steaks, pulled open his tracksuit pants, and dropped the tray in. To be sure the meat wouldn't slip, he made adjustments to tuck the tray into the top of his underpants.

She didn't see what else went into the groceries after that. The idea of eating anything that had been down his sweaty underpants was just too disgusting.

Back at the house she noticed there were cut-up pieces of bath towels on almost every surface. On benches, draped over the arms and backs of chairs, in piles here and there on the floor. The cemetery worker couldn't help but ask, he had a pointy nose that liked to poke and find out information.

"I have a condition," the sweaty one explained, "I sweat all the time." As he said this he picked up a piece of towel from the nearby bench, wiped his wet face, chest and underarms with it, and dropped the used towelling on the floor where he stood.

Where had she landed? Could she really stay here? The smell of the house was enough to send her packing. She didn't remember any towel scraps when she had come to look at the house, and it had smelt a lot better than it now did. I will give it a week or two, she thought, see how it goes.

True to his word, the sweaty one served up steak for dinner. There was no way she could eat meat from his underpants, but she couldn't let him know that either. Quietly retreating to her room with the dinner plate, she scooped the contents into a rubbish bag she could dispose of later. The other housemate ate the meat.

"It has been cooked," he reasoned, "what germs can survive that?"

A week or so later a man she had met at her aunt's and become friends with came to take her out for a meal. It had been a long and exciting week at fashion school and she was keen to see a bit of Melbourne. Sure, that would be fun! They went to the most amazing Indian curry house. Amazing to her because the food was made to true cultural recipes, not homogenised to suit the somewhat boring Australian tastes she had grown up with in Tasmania. Her eyes watered, she laughed, enjoying the company and the incredible food.

"This is the best Indian food in Melbourne," her date announced gleefully before shoving a large serve into his mouth. She began to feel excited about all she had to explore, taste and experience in this huge city. He drove her back to her house, stopping in his car until he saw her safely in the door. Her senses were on alert. Raised, angry male voices were coming from inside the house. Stepping into the shadows, she listened.

The sweaty man and another whose voice she did not recognise were arguing over a drug deal. Apparently the sweaty man owed a lot of money and couldn't pay. Then the unthinkable. She thought she misheard him.

"Take the girl, she hasn't been here long, no one will miss her. She's young, a hot little piece," her flatmate said.

The girl? Surely he doesn't mean me?

"Girl? How old?" asked the voice she did not recognise.

"Twenty-one or so. She's got a bit of life in her." They both laughed.

"Where is she?" asked the unknown voice.

"She's out, come back in the morning."

"All right, but don't fuck me around. If she's not here, it's you we'll be coming for."

She went back to the car. Shaking with emotion, she tried to act calm.

"You know I don't want to be alone tonight. Do you think you could stay? I don't have a bed for you, but we could top and tail?" She needed him to understand she was not offering sex, but she didn't want to tell him she was too scared to go to sleep in case they came for her.

They got as comfortable as they could on the single mattress she had on the floor. She didn't sleep much. When she did sleep, she imagined men coming into her room, picking her up off the floor and carrying her off to who knows what. Did people really sell women to pay their drug deals? This is crazy, surely they aren't serious?

Chapter 16

∽ **Crossing the Line** ∾

Whether or not the men would come back, she wasn't going to be there waiting. She got up early in the morning, surprised to find the cemetery worker in the kitchen reading the rental ads.

"I can't stay here," he explained, "this house, him."

She jumped at the opportunity, quick to say, "I'll move with you, let's find a house together!"

She had to get out of the house, so she went out for breakfast and waited. The familiar terror took over her body. Her voice became small, quiet. Hands shook as she tried to hold a coffee cup. She was hungry, but couldn't bring herself to eat. The need to cry was overwhelming. How could this be happening? It didn't make any sense. Was it safe to go back to the house?

The cemetery worker was true to his word. He signed a lease on a house nearby, vowing not to let the sweaty man know the address. Together they filled her little car, and in a few loads had moved to the empty, but clean-smelling house. That was a close call! She felt like she had been pulled from the jaws of a shark at the very last moment. All the fear, the dread, and then at the very last minute, saved from the pain.

Another housemate was soon found and the three settled in. It was a little farther to walk home from class now, and it meant she had to walk through a park in the evening. The park was mainly well-maintained lawn, with plenty of trees, concrete paths cutting through from one side to the other.

In the evening, as the days grew shorter heading out of summer, it was quite dark by the time she walked home after evening classes. Don't be afraid, she told herself, you don't want to draw attention to yourself.

But she was afraid. Any moment a man might jump out from behind a tree, from behind a bush. The long shadows that stretched out from the greenery gave her the creeps. She would walk as fast as she could, clutching a heavy satchel full of books. Most nights she only made it to halfway before she broke into a fast run, going hell for leather diagonally across the park to get to the footpath and welcoming street lights on the other side.

An old boyfriend came for a short visit, bringing with him her cat, Sam, and Madge, the little dog she had adopted a year back. And then he was gone. The friend who had stayed with her the night she thought she might be sold for drugs kept visiting. He spent quite a bit of time with her, didn't rush her to commit to more.

She was enjoying her studies, but living on the student allowance was pretty tough. She applied for jobs, but rarely got an interview, never mind a job offer. If she managed to get an interview she invariably got so nervous she became flustered, her words coming out in a funny order, her face flushing all prickly red and hot.

The father of the baby she had lost paid a visit. Life was good for him now, he explained. His wife had given birth again, and he had found God. Really found God, in a life-altering, let it completely take your life over kind of way. She felt happy for him. It wasn't the kind of life she would want, but he seemed to have grown tremendously in confidence and was a loyal and loving husband.

Looking into his eyes she felt the connection as strong as ever, but changed. It caused her great pain to watch him drive away, knowing she might never see him again. Standing outside in the dark, pulling her coat around her for warmth as he drove off, she felt terribly alone.

Would she ever know what it felt like to really be loved, adored, to feel safe, to have someone waiting just to see her at the end of the day and know it would last?

She could not say how the thought came to her. No one would employ her, but she had one thing she knew men wanted. They take it anyway, what's the difference, she reasoned silently. Answering an advertisement in a newspaper, she dressed herself up as though going to a job interview, then took the train into the city.

"This is a high-class establishment," the manager explained, "we don't take waifs and strays."

The woman's voice, everything about her, said, "Don't mess with me." She was well-dressed, with hair beautifully done and slightly garish nail polish on her finger nails. She seemed very firm. The wide-eyed girl felt as though the woman could see straight through her, could see how frightened and pathetic she really felt.

"Security is top notch. We expect you to be clean at all times. You turn up on time and if you don't show, you get three strikes and you're out. You will be going for regular health checks and we pay at the end of every day," the woman continued.

She heard herself agree. With hands that shook only slightly, she took the information that was offered.

"You'll probably want to use a different name," the manager stated. Yes, yes, she will.

She is shown the office, the reception and the waiting room. There is a lot of red. Red wallpaper, red carpet, giving a slightly cave-like feel. The air is thick with cigarette smoke.

In the waiting room an older woman, at least in her forties, stretches out a ridiculously long arm in greeting. She extends an equally long leg before standing up, giving the impression of a contortionist. Her waxing has clearly been very thorough, as the thong she wears to cover her pubic area is incredibly narrow and yet there is not a hair to be seen.

Looking upwards, the wide-eyed girl admires the woman's flat, firm belly, leading up to medium-sized breasts, contained in a bra as skimpy as the thong. She gives her own hand in greeting, wondering if she could ever be as intriguing as this woman.

Glancing around the room, trying desperately not to stare, she sees two other girls who look about her age, early to mid-twenties at most. Neither has the confident swagger of the thonged woman, but each has their own beauty.

One, with long light brown hair falling in curls around her breasts, looks bored. She reclines in a dress that could have been modest, covering right up to her collarbone and down past her knees, with long flowing sleeves. The green lace however, with no lining fabric underneath, made the intimate details of her flesh easily visible. Nipples pushed through the lace. Firm, full breasts were easily visible. A green thong barely contained her private area. She continued to file her nails, stopping to look up and smile, but was not interested in conversation.

"You're sure then? Many don't come back, you know. It's up to you," the manager said casually.

"Yes, I think so," the wide-eyed girl replied, although she wasn't really sure at all.

"You might want to get a wig then," continued the manager, "you have a distinctive face. Those big eyes would be hard to forget. Unless you don't mind people knowing. Up to you."

She did mind, very much.

On the train home she questioned why she was thinking of doing this. The money, she desperately needed the money. Why not ask for help, a loan? She had been raised to never ask for money. Money was a truly dirty word in her mother's house. She remembered too the occasions when Nanna could not help, so in desperation Mum had made the phone call to Grandma, in Sydney. Grandma generally provided what was asked for, but not before taking the time to completely humiliate Mum and leave her in tears on the other end of the phone.

The old bastard, Nanna's husband, hadn't been much better. Not long ago, before she had moved to Melbourne, he had sent a letter to Mum asking her to repay a small sum of about $3000 that Nanna had loaned to Mum before her sudden death. Mum did not take kindly to his request. To the wide-eyed girl's horror, she had quickly penned a reply to him.

"Dear ___, in light of your inappropriate relationship with my daughters whilst they were in your care, I don't think any further communication with you is appropriate."

Did this mean that after pretending not to believe her daughters through all the years they complained about his sleazy attentions, she had believed them, had known the whole time? Had it just been inconvenient to have them live at home with her? Both girls asked her these questions, but she refused to answer.

Instinct suggested one answer, but it was more than either girl could own. Mum couldn't have betrayed them so badly, could she? If she did, was she even aware of it? She was pretty off the rails during those years, but even so? Asking for money became linked to everything unpleasant, sexual abuse, betrayal and loss. She was never going to ask for money.

The next day she went shopping. What kind of underwear would she need? Black, lacy, sexy. And a wig! She couldn't believe how easily she found a wig shop. Oddly she found it exciting. The wig was a deep red shade, a bob cut with a solid, straight fringe and she rather liked it.

As she posed in the shop, making her decision, she revelled in her anonymity. No one would know who she was!

She had been stalked for so long, intimate details of her life under his microscope. She shuddered involuntarily at the thought of the Stalker getting off on the underwear he had stolen from her. Pushing down sudden tears and the horrific memories that caused them, she dragged herself back to the moment.

Gazing at her face, somehow cheekier and more vibrant under the fabulous wig, she felt how fully delicious it was to be so completely anonymous! She needed new lipstick, and it had to match the wig. Then inspiration struck! She could go home and make a see-through dress, she had a few metres of a fabulous, incredibly light black sheer fabric.

Chapter 17

∽ **Cigarettes and Minties** ∾

The journey home on the train was a nervous one. Her courage had shrunk by now. In the bags she clutched lay her rent money – transformed into lingerie and a fabulous red wig.

Dressed in jeans and sneakers as she made her way into the city for her first shift a few days later, she was completely inconspicuous. She was nervous, but smiled at the thought that no one on the train would ever have guessed where she was going or what she was about to do.

Arriving, she found herself whisked upstairs to change. The bathroom was long. A mirror extended the length of it, allowing six or seven girls at once to stand in front of it and repair their appearance. She applied a lot of makeup, covering her face as best she could.

She had worn heels, but they did not compare to the magnificent red stilettos of the long-armed, long-legged woman she had met the day she had come for an interview. They got talking. This woman was friendly, professional, and certainly seemed to know the ropes. Wide-eyed girl listened intently as she undressed, then dressed. Looking at herself in the mirror she was surprised to see how flat her own belly was. Not taut and muscular like her long-armed colleague, but flat and soft, almost a little childlike.

Underwear in place, dress on, makeup complete, she reached for the wig. Sitting on its plastic stand it seemed to be waiting for her to decide, would she carry through or not? Pushing every doubt down as far as she could, she reached for the wig. Settling it, a little too tightly at first as she didn't want it to move, she stood back to admire her work.

"Don't forget your smokes," one of the younger girls called to her, "you'll be wanting them."

Paying more attention as she followed her new friends down the hallway, she noticed a number of rooms. Doors open, she peered in to see each had a bed, a shower, some had a spa. The décor was shocking, lots of red, gold, all the colours you might expect in such a place. Moving down the stairwell she felt faint. What if someone chose her? No, no one would.

The waiting room was small, with couches around three walls. The girls perched themselves on the couches, lit cigarettes and waited. The television was switched on. She observed them. Their body language, their make-up, everything about them fascinated her. How had they all ended up in here?

"Minty?" asked the girl in the see-through green dress. "You'll grow to like these," she said, "they drown out the taste of the smokes a bit."

"Does everybody here smoke?" asked the wide-eyed girl.

"Pretty much," was the answer. She pulled out her own and lit up.

For the next hour they exchanged pleasantries, chatted a little. She discovered the girl in the green dress was studying at university and found this a great way to pay her bills. Another was financing her drug addiction, "but don't tell the boss that, no drugs allowed here, they check, you know."

The older woman with the long arms didn't speak much. She filed her nails, ate Minties, smoked cigarettes and waited.

The first man to enter the room was no match for the charms of the long-armed woman. Her confident enthusiasm made his eyes sparkle. He barely glanced at the other women in the room before taking her hand and leading her to reception to pay. She cheekily offered him a few extras, extracting a higher price with each. Looking back, she winked naughtily at the waiting room as she went.

Panic rose in her stomach. What if he had chosen her? Oh shit, what will I do? And then another man was standing in front of them. This one took his time, surveying them all as though it was a terribly important decision.

Her name was called, but she did not respond. She had forgotten the false name she had chosen. The girl beside her nudged her, looking at her with great compassion. The girls told her later that they thought she was going to bolt, out into the street in her underwear, rather than go with him.

But she didn't run. She allowed herself to be led to the payment area, then led the man up the stairs. Silently in her head she ran through the instructions she had been given as they walked toward the room she had been assigned. First room on the right. Make him undress and get him in the shower to wash. Don't forget to look and make sure he hasn't got crabs or anything nasty down there.

All taken care of, now what?

Nervous, fumbling as he lay on the bed and beckoned her to join him, she confessed.

"I haven't done this before, I'm not sure."

"Oh, come on!" the man exclaimed, his grey beard twitching in annoyance. "I'm not paying for a bloody virgin, and I'm sure you're not one. Are you going to get on with it?"

She should have left then. But she didn't. Remembering what the girls told her, how they had shown her, she opened the condom packet, took the condom and placed it in her mouth. Somehow, she managed to apply it to him, whilst unbeknown to him applying a very generous amount of lubrication. If she couldn't feel it, she could do it. She had spent most of her childhood learning how not to feel, how to disassociate from men, from her true feelings. She had this.

It was over fast. She found it revolting. The way he moved, the noises he made as he peaked. Disgusting. When he was done she showered herself, dressed, then waited while he showered again before dressing.

She felt peculiar, but not in a way she could describe. She was different now. She had well and truly crossed the line and would never be the same again.

As he made his way downstairs ahead of her, he didn't look back, as though he too was disassociating himself from the act. In a moment he was back out on the street and she was back on the couch, being congratulated by her colleagues for not doing a runner.

Later, on the train ride home, she looked about the carriage, avoiding eye contact with her fellow commuters. Riding into town that morning she had smiled, connected with people, confident not a soul knew where she was going or what she was about to do. Now, at the end of the day, her shame was so great she could not look at any of them, convinced if she did they would know exactly what she had done.

It would be some years before she would understand that it was not so much shame for her experiences, for what she had done, that kept her prisoner. In reality, she was not ashamed, nor did she really feel women, or men, working in that industry should be.

She was scared of being found out. Scared to the marrow of her bone. Scared of how people would react if they ever found out what she had done. Would her family still love her? What would her friends say? Would she have any friends left if they found out? The journey to the place where she is accepting of her truth, of who she is and the many experiences that led towards her own acceptance and the courage to speak it, would take her well into her forties.

Along that road to finding her voice, her courage, she occasionally shared her truth and was surprised to discover how many women harboured similar secrets.

"Only once, like a one-night stand but he paid. I didn't really need the money, I was just curious," one woman told her.

"I only did it when I couldn't make my rent," another confessed.

The one thing all who shared their confessions with her had in common was the somewhat toxic shame that their desperate need for no one to know created within them.

Chapter 18

Shame and Redemption

Fear and shame were nothing new for her. She had simply added one more layer. She did go back, one day a week, a couple of clients a day. She could manage that. This world was so shocking, so new, she wished she could take a camera and interview them all. The girls, the punters, the bosses.

There was nothing shocking in the way people behaved toward each other. The shock was how she could possibly ever explain herself if anyone ever found out. Here she found people willing to defend each other. People who did not judge her for being poor, for talking too much, for not talking enough, for not being good at making friends.

Here at least there was honesty. Men paid for sex, pure and simple. There was no pretence of wanting relationship, pretending to care long enough to get what they wanted. She had always felt deeply ashamed, tarnished and unworthy. Now she had no one to blame but herself.

The last shift she did a young man had come in, a man her age. What would he need to be in a place like this for? He was a good-looking man, super confident, a touch arrogant. Surely he could pull a girl any night of the week?

He chose her. She panicked. Older men she could deal with, but not this. She managed to disassociate enough to do what was asked of her, but it shook her badly. She shouldn't be here, she should be out making the life she dreamed of. She was a fashion student, she was going to be famous – yet here she was bouncing on a man she didn't know and feeling like she might die of self-disgust.

This was only her fourth shift. One of them she had spent on the couch without even attracting a punter! Imagine being in that position and being knocked back! During her time on the couch she listened, asked questions. Through the other women she began to understand her own truth for the first time. She wasn't here because she needed the money, she was here because of the abuse. Because of the bullying.

The deep sadness in her heart lightened somewhat as she sat on the couch, minty sticking her teeth together as she listened to the stories. She met only one woman who did not talk of her experiences of childhood sexual abuse. Rape, beatings, control. It was all about control.

She needed to stop being the victim to the abuse she had experienced and take control. That realisation carried her out of there for the last time, although she did not know that yet. Home. She made it home, safe and sound. No one need ever know. For the first time in some years she fell asleep that night without fear, a smile relaxing her face.

The next day the boyfriend she had left in Hobart called. She hadn't heard from him in a long time, their connection had not been strong when she left. He had a new girlfriend, he just wanted to tell her himself. Something in her snapped and the tears fell hard and fast. He was rejecting her! Christ, he didn't even know what she had been doing. What would he think if he knew? What would everyone think? Another girlfriend. She reacted angrily, unreasonably. They weren't together so what was she so upset about? The cemetery worker was surprised.

"You have another boyfriend, here, what's the problem? I can't see anything wrong here. Why do you care?" he asked.

But she did care. She wasted some of the precious money she had earned on a flight and went home to Hobart for the weekend. He wasn't home, had gone away for the weekend with his girlfriend. She spent the weekend with her family and friends, complaining about him. Dad took her to the airport.

"There's something very wrong here. You seem odd. You don't really care about this girlfriend, do you?" Dad stated, rather than asked.

"No," she sputtered through the tears that came unbidden but with force. No, she didn't. Dad pulled the car to the side of the road and waited.

"It's just that… Dad, I've done something stupid."

Dad handed her his favourite green hanky.

"Dad, imagine the worst thing your daughter could do, the worst job. I've been doing it," she sobbed. Dad didn't raise an eyebrow. A tear escaped him as he watched her. He reached out a hand to take hers.

"We're going to the bank. Just hold on a minute," Dad instructed gently.

Dad pulled the car back onto the road and drove to the city, to his bank's automatic cash machine. Without another word he got out, made his transaction, then came back to the car with a wad of cash rolled up.

"It's all I've got," he stated, "I've been saving for a new car."

"I can't take that, Dad! No way!"

"You can, and you will. You won't be doing that work anymore. If you need more I will find a way to get it to you. Just take it."

Dad, the man who had always borrowed from her, was giving her his savings. It was nearly five hundred dollars. Not much to most, but everything to him.

She cried all the way to the airport. Life with Dad hadn't been easy. But among all the painful memories, she also had memories of Dad that were good. The way he read stories to her when she was young. Standing out on the cold, concrete floor, beside her in the garage as he made wooden toys for sale. His hands guiding hers as he taught her to use hand chisels, sanding blocks, and how to oil the wood. Those memories, the way she loved him even in the midst of his abuse, flooded through her now as the tears dripped from her chin.

She took the money. Dad had come to her rescue. Not one word of judgment. His face showed nothing but love and compassion. She already knew Dad was a vault. No one kept secrets as well as he did. She was safe.

Safety is a relative state. Arriving home, she settled into student life once more. She had Dad's money and some of the money she had earned tucked away. Her mind wandered often to the brothel, the memories, and she floated between the delicious sense of empowerment she had never known before and the cold, gnawing fear that someone would find out.

Her shame came not so much from what she had done, but from her fear of what others would think of her if she were discovered. At times the fear of being discovered was overwhelming, and she wished so desperately she had not gone down that path.

Chapter 19

～ **Betrayal** ～

Sam the cat wasn't doing well. He had been a little off his food the last twenty-four hours and quieter than usual. He didn't seem too steady on his feet either, and blood had begun trickling from a small wound behind his ear. She took him to the vet and soon discovered not only had Sam been bitten by a large dog, the bite had introduced a pathogen that stopped his blood from clotting. Sam was given injections and sent home to rest.

By the next afternoon Sam was crying, lying on the bed she had made for him in the lounge room. The third flatmate scooped up Sam and they ran to the car. Crying hard, it wasn't easy to see where she was going, but she drove as best she could. Don't die, Sam, please don't die.

"There's not much we can do," the vet explained, "not without a blood transfusion." She learned that a blood transfusion would normally occur once the donor cat's blood had been screened. If it was not a match the transfusion would swiftly kill Sam, rather than cure him.

They called a cat shelter. Was it possible one of their healthy cats could give blood? Absolutely not, was the answer.

Sam was a very big cat. To allow him to stretch out, the vet placed him on the floor in a cage normally inhabited by large dogs. She sat with him, stroking his paw, under his chin, his beautiful face, hoping the drip in his leg didn't hurt him too much. Sam was unconscious now, unresponsive to her attentions.

Heartbroken she went home, to wait. The phone rang early the next morning.

"I can't say for sure," said the vet, "but I am hopeful." He explained that another cat had come for a routine check-up and his owner had seen Sam and wanted to help.

"She is here now, and has given permission for her cat to give blood in a direct transfusion. Sam is very weak, he has been bleeding through the night, we haven't got long. If we don't do this, he will die. If we do, he may still die. If the blood is a match though, he has a chance," the vet explained. More tears, struggling to speak through them, she gives permission.

"Yes, please try, yes!" She thinks the vet promises to call later but she doesn't really hear anything now. She just has to wait.

Lunchtime. She hasn't gone to school. Hasn't left the house. She sits in her room, listening to Bowie's song, 'Heroes,' and waits. Finally the phone rings!

"I don't want to get your hopes up," said the vet, "but he survived the transfusion. He has opened his eyes. He is still very weak, so the next twenty-four hours will be crucial."

At the vet clinic she sat with him, holding his paw, urging him to get strong. He did, and so did the bill. Thanks to Dad and her brief sojourn at the brothel, she managed to pay most of the bill. The rest she would pay off over time.

She didn't care about losing the money, she was overjoyed to be taking Sam home. His care would require an iron-rich diet and special supplements for some time, but she didn't care. She would go without to take care of him.

And then the hammer dropped. By now the friend who had saved her from the drug dealers, although he didn't know it at the time, was staying over regularly. She enjoyed his company, his sense of humour, his solidity. They weren't intimate yet, but that might come. The last shift she had done at the brothel she had arrived home late. He had phoned, repeatedly, worried that something was wrong. She remembered telling him not to worry, she had just been in the city having a coffee and lost track of the time.

Unbeknown to her, this had aroused the curiosity of the cemetery worker.

"Where have you been going?" he asked, "and the wig – what's with that?" His tone, his expression, told her he knew. How? How could he have known? Yes, he had seen the wig, but he hadn't asked any questions at the time.

She felt she could trust him, after all, apart from that experience she kept no secrets. He had provided food when her budget ran out, helped care for Sam and Madge the dog. She could trust him. Heart a-flutter, she told him. Everything. She was surprised how relieved she felt to share it.

He didn't say much, just let her talk. As she finished, head down in deep contemplation, she felt his hand on her thigh. Looking up she was surprised to see him smiling at her lecherously.

"Perhaps then, you would consider sleeping with me? If you can sleep with men you don't know for money, then surely you can share with your friends?"

And in a flash her momentary safety was shattered.

"Well at least think about it," the cemetery worker snapped, before leaving the room. She thought about it alright! No way was she doing that. She had thought he was different, didn't just see her for sex. Fool, why did you tell him? Because he knew. He just wanted you to know that. And now, he has all the power and she has none.

She did nothing for several days. Shame burning her alive, she avoided him. Is this what the rest of her life would be like?

She stayed in her room when she was at home and began looking for another share house. Late at night her bedroom door flung open. Glaring at her, he announced sharply that a decision had been made, he and the other flatmate would be moving out. She could have the house, and the lease, to herself.

For weeks she had been managing to keep her rent paid, pay her way, just. The idea of being left alone in the house and having to invite strangers in to share it with her was beyond terrifying. After a sleepless night she called the friend.

"We'll think of something," he promised. And he did.

Later that day he arrived. The cemetery worker and other flatmate were both out, so working quickly they packed everything into her car and his, including of course the cat and the dog, and they drove away. She knew the cemetery worker had no desire to move, he was just trying to force her to either move or give him what he wanted. She didn't really care about any of that, she just missed her friend. She was devastated by the difference in both his opinion of her and his treatment of her, once he knew.

A few suburbs away, she unpacked what she needed at the home of her boyfriend's father.

"The old man's away for a few months," he informed her. It was an older style house, and it looked and smelt of old people. The teapot, breadbin, crocheted things here and there. But it was home for a while. The friend was working away from Melbourne, so was soon in his car and headed back to work. This was going to be tricky, no fenced yard for the dog. However, her aunt's house was only a short walk away and that gave her great comfort.

In the days together in his father's house, they became closer. Close enough to develop a relationship. There were a few alarm bells, but she refused to listen to her inner guidance. Together, they found a room in a share house. She should really have moved on her own, but her confidence was shattered. Before long the alarm bells rang true. She discovered his jealous streak. She found him a bit unnerving when he was angry, had a sense he might not be fully in control of his actions. One night, when she was late home from fashion school, time stopped.

Their flatmate, a gregarious teacher and artist, was excited. His cousin from overseas was visiting. Did they want to go out for a drink with her? Sure, yes! That would be fun! It wasn't, for they never got there. The boyfriend, enraged with jealousy, chased her around the house, yelling abuse at her, calling her names. The flatmate and his cousin beat a hasty retreat and waited, out in the street.

She hid, as she had done as a child running from her father, in a neighbour's driveway. Imagine her horror as the angry boyfriend came down that driveway looking for her. As quickly and quietly as she could, the wide-eyed girl inched her body underneath the car she had been hiding behind.

Don't see me, please don't see me! She silently begged the owners of the car not to come out of their house, not to see her lest they might give her away.

He ranted, called her filthy names, demanding she come out of hiding.

Thankfully no one came out of the house. She watched his feet turn and walk away after seconds that felt like years. Her heartbeat deafening in her ears, she remained under the car for some time, not moving until she was sure she heard him return to their own house and shut the front door behind him.

Chapter 20

～ The Safe Motorbike ～

Eventually everyone except the boyfriend found a taxi and left. Her aunt called, said the boyfriend had called her, worried. What had gone on? Was she okay? She tried to explain, but felt ashamed, embarrassed.

"Stay here with us. He says he will move out, then you can go home," her aunt offered.

So she did. But she felt awkward and foolish. She didn't know how to apologise. You don't have to, her flatmate encouraged, it wasn't your fault. But perhaps it was. Perhaps she did not love him enough and he felt it. Did she? She was scared of him, she knew that. And she would not lie with someone she was afraid of.

But she did need to take responsibility, for her intuition had told her to move on her own and she had refused to listen because she was afraid.

Then life got busy. A local high school that served under-privileged teenagers of the area was being forced to close. It was to be repackaged as a government-run school, but one for privileged girls, one parents would pay good money to send their girls to. Outraged, the flatmate and many other socially minded souls began a sit-in protest. They moved into the school and stayed. She believed in their cause, this school was so important to the local kids. Many had parents battling with drugs, addiction and behavioural issues that made it hard for their kids. So she joined in. It was summer holidays. No school now until university started in the New Year.

That was where she met the policeman. He wasn't one of the ones who followed orders and marched on the sitting protestors, hitting them with batons while yelling in unison, "Move! Move! Move!" He wasn't present when their batons hit women, grandmothers, children. Nor did he see the blood on the faces, arms and bodies of the peaceful protestors. Pigs' blood, the newspapers would say later that day, the protestors threw pigs blood on themselves so they could scream police brutality. She had seen no evidence of that. All she saw was peaceful, sitting protestors being hit so hard they bled.

In the days before this she had begun talking with the policeman. He seemed quite nice, not what she expected. Her experiences with police in the past hadn't been very positive. Most had been nice enough to her, but the laws that bound them had meant they could do nothing to help her. She was curious about this man. He was at least ten or more years older, but she didn't mind that. He felt nice to stand next to. His eyes twinkled. When he laughed his whole face screwed up. She couldn't talk for long.

"We don't want to be seen," he joked, "you or me, consorting with the enemy!"

She had met him later, just to talk. A date? On your motorbike? Why not, she had never been on a bike, but she remembered her mother loved it. Before they could go on the date the violence with the batons happened. She told her flatmate about the date. His face said it all.

"Would you rather I didn't tell you?" she asked.

"No, I would rather you didn't go. How could you?" He meant it. She went. The policeman was nice, tall, a little overweight, he had a gentleness about him that was very appealing. She found his more mature presence very comforting.

He introduced her to riding, dressing her up in leather pants, jacket and a helmet. The helmet she understood was required, but she didn't like it. With it crammed on her head she felt claustrophobic, unsafe. She didn't like being contained, caged in. She didn't like either that she had limited vision, only able to see out through the visor. What if someone was to come up behind her? She wouldn't know until it was too late. You're on a fast-moving motorbike! Seriously, no one is going to sneak up behind you.

Heart racing, she climbed on, listened to his instructions.

"Hold on, just let your body move with mine, don't resist, relax, don't worry if you go to sleep." Go to sleep – not likely! She'd fall off, wouldn't she?

Shit! Too late. She is holding on for dear life, arms wrapped firmly around his waist. Soon she realises her eyes are closed. Big breath. She opens her eyes. Things look as they do when she is driving her car, only she feels far less disconnection from the ground, from the road surface. It feels as if she could almost reach out and touch the buildings, cars and people they fly past. This is a little like flying.

Flying. As a child she was convinced she could fly. She remembers being young, racing around the yard at home as fast as she could, then leaping into the air. Arms outstretched, she could almost feel herself moving gracefully upwards. Eyes sparkling with hope as she looked upward to the sky. Then the painful thud as she hit the ground. She always, always hit the ground, but she kept trying, until her parents stopped her.

"People will think you are mad. You don't want to be locked up, do you?" they had threatened.

Relaxing into the ride, she became aware of her body moving freely with his, no longer staying rigid and fighting his. The ride became smooth. She began to trust, enjoying the sensation and the sense of freedom she was beginning to feel.

"Just let your body go," he had instructed. Laughing in her helmet, unheard by anyone but her, she realised she had had no idea what that meant! How do you just "let your body go?" Go where? What would that feel like?

"Trust," she whispered, "it feels like trust."

Their relationship was brief, but exciting, yet also comforting and safe. It was he who broke it off. Her father and stepmother had come to visit for a week.

"I don't like who you are around them," the policeman said, "I don't like this you. You are a bit rough around them."

"Perhaps," she said quietly, caught off guard. She hadn't seen this coming, thought she had found a safe haven, emotionally and physically. She was devastated, but let him go. Two days later he returned, pulling his car into the driveway and stepping out with the most serious face she had seen on him.

"I'll go inside," said Dad, "hear him out." She did. They cried, embraced, and he apologised.

"I made a mistake," he said, "can we forget this and go back to normal?"

"No," she said, "I can't. Think what you like of my father, God knows I haven't always liked him. But Dad has supported me when no one else is willing to. You really hurt me."

She didn't want to watch him go. The hurt in his face hit her hard, made her want to run after him. But she didn't. She didn't like being hurt and she couldn't trust him now, she knew that in a second her world built around him might crumble and she couldn't risk that.

He had encouraged her to join the army reserves. That way, he had said, you can earn money while you study and meet new people, it's worth a try. He had been spot on! She joined and trained as a medic. The training was hard, she wasn't used to carrying heavy packs, and her map reading skills were shocking. She passed that test though. The day she had been supposed to lead her fellow trainees back to their water-logged camp on a rainy day at Puckapunyal, she had stopped walking, and turned to the corporal to say, "I give up, I have no idea where we are!"

As she turned, a camouflage fabric backpack caused her to fall forward. She landed awkwardly on all fours, suddenly very aware of the foot she had twisted a little the day before. Looking around she saw the tents, not much more than fabric tethered to trees really. No way! She had no idea how, but she had led them back to the camp. Standing up, hands by her side in the soldierly way, she announced, "We're here, Corporal!"

The corporal shook his head, laughter all over his young face.

"I don't know how you did it, I think we all know it's just a lucky break, but yes, you got us home and I am going to have to pass you." That was a relief! She would have been kicked out of the reserves before she really started if she had failed this test. What a great feeling it was to pass!

Chapter 21

∽ Madge ∽

A little while after her return home from training, a corporal she had met there attended the meeting of her unit one Tuesday evening. She had felt drawn to him. His nature was not as harsh as some, and he had helped her avoid punishment for losing her hat, forgetting her weapon, everything was punishable in training. The punishments weren't terrible, they were designed to help recruits pay more attention, as they would need to be alert and aware should they see live action. Most often her punishment had involved having to stay up in the night and walk the perimeter with another recruit. She had done a lot of walking!

There he was in her mess hall at the end of training that night. His eyebrows raised as she entered the room. She was surprised to see him, nervous at first. Her unit didn't treat her like a recruit. She had to follow protocols, raise her hand in salute at the appropriate moments and pay attention to hierarchy, but her unit were mainly friendly and encouraging and she enjoyed working with them. Perhaps she would like to see a movie with him? Can they do that, she asks, would it get them into trouble? Just a movie, should be no problem, he assured her.

They went out a few times, getting to know each other. He was closer to her age. She met his family, they approved. He moved briefly into her share house with her, before they moved together to a smaller apartment. She only had the cat now, for Madge had gone for treatment and never returned. During the school protest she had met a volunteer from a public animal hospital and shelter. Much as she had begged, they would not look at Madge without a fee, and she could not pay.

Madge, a small little dog with a long, wiry black coat, was not happy unless she was right beside her. When she went out, Madge would climb fences and roam the neighbourhood to find her. So she left Madge in her room when she went out. Food, water, bed. But Madge of course had other ideas and spent her alone time in the girl's bed.

Imagine a little dog, riddled with allergic reactions, skin flaking off in little pieces on every surface she touched. Hearing the little dog's cries as the irritation drove her to despair was heart breaking. Little bits of blood and ooze spread wherever she lay. The wide-eyed girl kept a sheet over her bed during the day. Madge's digestive system was in crisis too, adding to her physical distress with vomiting and diarrhea. She didn't like the mess, but she could work around it. What broke her heart was the state of her Madge. She had done all she could with the vets, but the treatments were expensive and not working, so she felt she had run out of options.

"I can take her," her friend said, "if I say she is a stray they will look after her, get her well, then I can bring her back." She cried, tears dripping onto Madge, whose little chest was pressed against hers, small head on her shoulder. The brown eyes that looked at her with such love and trust. What else could she do? Madge needed help, she couldn't give it.

"Go on then, take her." Her friend took Madge in his arms. She wriggled, looking back with big eyes. Madge squealed as he walked away with her. Did she know they would never see each other again?

"They might not let me bring her back," he said, "are you sure?"

"No," she wanted to yell, "no, I'm bloody not!" But what she said was entirely different.

"Yes," she said, "yes." She knew Madge was extremely unwell and there was nothing she could do about it. Sobbing, she stood on the street, watching the car drive away. Her heart felt like it was shredded as she saw her beloved Madge's face appear at the back window of the car.

Her small, pointy little feet were scratching at the glass. Before she could run after them, do anything, the car was around the corner and gone. Madge was gone. And it was her fault.

How could she do this to Madge? What if they didn't look after her? What if she wasn't adopted by someone who had the money to care for her better? What if she was euthanised? What ifs, that was all she had now of the dear little dog who had loved her so much. Back inside the house she kept busy cleaning, vacuuming, and washing. Cleaning the flaky skin, the blood spots, every little bit of Madge's pain was washed out of their room. If only life were different. If only she weren't so different. But she was.

She was awkward and shy, she felt ashamed, dirty and unworthy, she always had, even though she wasn't sure why. Her recent actions hadn't helped this. Now it wasn't just what others had done to her, but what she had chosen to do to herself that caused great shame.

At least Madge didn't die like the cats before Sam had, murdered by the cruel Stalker. Madge had a chance. In the years that followed, when her memories danced back to the day she sent Madge away, she was overwhelmed with grief and guilt. If only she had been able to ask for help.

Following is understanding that came, more than twenty years later:

Shame! Shame on you. You should be ashamed. I have known shame for as long as I can remember. Shamed into being quiet. Shamed because my parents were poor. We aren't welcome, Mum would say of her family, they just put up with us because they must. We're poor, they don't want us at their parties.

Mum never felt good enough for her family. But my experience of her family did not match with her beliefs, I wanted to be part of the tribe. Her eldest brother, my beautiful uncle, sent the money for me to attend the film and television school, yet I was asked to not speak of this, not acknowledge it. I still don't know why. I do know Mum actually loved her family very much, and they her, but her own shame, deep inside her, made her feel heartbreakingly unlovable.

The never spoken of rape that my family would say never happened to me, that filled me with shame so deep it tainted everything. From that moment, I forgot how it felt to feel "normal," accepted, worthy of the attention of another. I withdrew into a world of books, escaping to the world of Narnia, the Famous Five. I began drawing, mainly animals, and Nanna taught me to paint. On the outside I appeared normal, bright and talkative to the point of being annoying. On the inside, I felt such deep shame I could not express.

After the rape, I became constipated. This lasted for several years. Going to the toilet hurt. I was terrified someone would find out. I felt I was being punished for the disgusting thing that had happened to me. I hated anyone hearing my pain as I sat on the toilet, but Mum's house wasn't very private. I would sit, teeth clenched, crying as I knew the pain to come when I relaxed.

I had little memory of the rape itself, my mind had carefully tucked it away until many years later when I would be able to deal with the full memory. I sat and cried, feeling disassociated from my family, dirty, in pain and ashamed.

Shame played out throughout my life, affecting most decisions in work, relationships and particularly family. I could have asked my aunt in Melbourne for help, rather than deepen my shame at the brothel. She would have helped, without hesitation. The fault was mine, not hers. I could not bear the shame of asking. My beautiful aunt had no idea of the shame I carried inside. Shame that lay buried deep, poisoning everything, but remaining invisible to most.

Shame that deep is like a plate-glass wall between you and everybody else. You can lean right up to the wall, breathe against it and feel your *warm breath as it creates a fog on the glass. But you can't pass through the wall, and no one else can reach you. Isolated, ashamed, you function in the world at a high enough level to convince everyone else you are okay, one of them. But you are not. You are eaten alive by shame.*

The tragedy is the shame should never have been yours. But you were too young to understand, too young to seek help, and too ashamed to tell another soul.

Chapter 22

❧ Ring Ring ☙

She and the corporal lasted some months together in the apartment, before the phone calls began. She didn't recognise the man's voice.

"I'm calling for him," the voice announced. She hung up. Although she had no idea who the voice belonged to, that one call was enough to terrify her. Not another one? How? She hadn't been talking on the radio for more than a year. Nothing had happened, her animals hadn't been hurt, wasn't she safe here?

The calls kept coming. Always when she was home alone. Oh shit, he knows there is no one here, it's just me. She began keeping the doors locked and the blinds drawn when she was home alone. Knowing he could not watch her inside the apartment made her feel a little safer. It was an old apartment, so the doors were quite solid, the windows thick and heavy, and she was grateful.

"Why are you doing this?" she demanded.

"I'm a friend, I'm calling for him," the voice would say. This voice didn't torment her about her movements during the day. Didn't threaten her in any obvious way. He didn't have to. Every call tapped in to the terror of years of being stalked and the murder of her cats. Then one grey afternoon, as she approached the backdoor of her apartment, her voice jammed in her throat and she forgot how to breathe.

On the doormat, completely separate from its body, was the head of a possum. Open eyes looked up at her, as if imploring her. In what seemed like a long distance away, she heard her voice, her screams. Scattered on the ground around the possum was the body, and all four of the severed legs. Breathing the shallow breath of one in shock, she made her way around the building to the front door. Her key wouldn't work in the lock.

Damn, she had forgotten the lock needed repair. Back she went. Staring at the horrific face looking up at her from the mat, she summoned the courage to lean over, unlock the door, push it open and leap over the possum into the sanctuary inside. Slamming the door shut behind her, she realised she had nothing to be afraid of. Sam was a big cat, and a farm cat. Sam liked to hunt. She cried now with relief! It wasn't a stalker, it was Sam who had done this! So where was Sam? In his favourite place, curled up in the armchair that got the afternoon sun. Sitting on the edge of the chair, stroking under his chin as he woke and stretched out beautiful, long silver-grey legs, she felt the full force of terror strike her.

Sam didn't kill the possum. Sam had been locked inside all day.

Lifting Sam and clutching him to her chest, she unconsciously began rocking her body back and forth, comforting herself as best she could while trying to deal with the knowledge she would have to also deal with the dismembered remains of the possum.

When her corporal boyfriend came home that night she told him about the possum, cried as she described placing her hands inside plastic bags to pick up the pieces and place them in the bin. She hadn't told him much about the stalking experience. Sharing it made her feel so pathetic, helpless. Since moving to Melbourne she hadn't needed to bring others into her fearful world. Now she had no choice. She talked to her superior the next day, and he went to work immediately on finding a solution.

Before anything could be organised, the caller made it easy for them. He couldn't resist boasting.

"I'm just around the corner in the phone box," he bragged. She walked to the phone box, stood in it, tried to imagine this new intruder in her life. What was he gaining from this? Apart from knowing she was scared? She went home and unplugged the phone. If that was his only means of contact, then she simply wouldn't answer it.

The relationship took a nosedive. She was no longer really present, as she was afraid most of the time now. She loved him, but she couldn't share everything with him.

He then sealed their fate.

"There's another way to have sex," he suggested, "some girls really like it." She didn't. Although she had not tried it, the idea of it revolted her and sent her into a panic. He persisted, gently, but persisted. Who was she to be a prude, she reasoned. Why not, how bad could it be?

It was over mercifully fast. Within moments she was in the bathroom, door locked, rocking back and forth as she sat on the toilet. Every ounce of shame she had ever felt hit her like a horrific tidal wave. Shame-fuelled tears flowed. Her heart ached so badly she wanted to open her mouth and let the noise out. Although she didn't, she could hear the sound her whole being wanted to make. A loud, low, guttural moan. The moan that expressed every aspect of the pain she had felt at seven. The memory of rape remained hidden, but the feelings from it hit her with full, familiar force. For some time she stayed, rocking, weeping, disappearing in the horror of fresh realisation.

Every time she looked at him she felt tremendous self-disgust, shame and disconnection. She withdrew, like a crab pulling itself back into the safety of its shell. He also pulled back from her, seeming to find television better company than her. Neither understood what was happening, nor had the maturity to attempt to find out.

Feeling she had failed once more, she asked him to move out, and he did. The phone calls hadn't started coming in again after she had left the phone unplugged for a few weeks. It was a relief to have the apartment to herself for a short while. She started to feel safe, as safe as she had ever felt at least, and advertised for a flatmate to move in and share the expenses. They got on well to start with, before she hooked up with a new boyfriend.

There was never much time between men. She could not bear the loneliness and fear, the toxic combination that left her terrified. She tried to be confident, sassy, sexy, all the things she felt she was not. But as much as she tried, she could never quite shake the fear that at any moment the Stalker might appear, silently behind her, and plunge the knife into her back. Or worse, she would return home one day to find Sam the cat pinned by a knife to her front door, or dismembered like the unlucky possum.

This new relationship was good! He was motivated, fit, positive and encouraged her to start her own business. She had begun creating patterns for teddy bears. Fashion school had finished some time back. She liked designing clothes, but knew she didn't have the extraordinary talent needed to make a big career out of it. She had worked at a job in the last year making patterns for a company, and it had not been pleasant. Most of her work involved making patterns for garments made by other companies. The boss would throw a garment on the table saying, "Make a pattern off this!" Bears were much more fun! It was such a challenge to create flat shapes on card that when sewn would provide the chubby legs, big toes and character filled faces she could see in her imagination.

Her mother was furious. This man was almost twice her age! She sent him a letter, a very unkind one, telling him he was too old, her daughter didn't want to be saddled with his children, how could he be so selfish? He was hurt by this. They shared a meal, drank wine, and eventually laughed at her mother's appalling, inappropriate behaviour. She kept the letter for some time. It helped to remind her, when she felt sad because her mother was not so easy to communicate with and was rarely as unconditionally supportive as Nanna had been, that this is how Mum was.

She loved Mum, but she couldn't always count on her to be there when she needed her. She didn't understand why Mum was like this. All she remembered was from when she was sixteen. Crying at Nanna's kitchen table, asking Nanna why her mother had behaved so badly towards her recently.

"She can't help it," Nanna had explained. "I can't say what it is about her, but it isn't your fault. You mustn't ever think it is your fault. Your Mum was born this way. She always reacted strangely to things, always. She just never feels good enough. She feels so bad about herself, she always has. You're not like her," Nanna had reassured.

But it hurt. She wanted a mother she could talk to, openly, honestly, without judgment. Mum did irrational reaction incredibly well. Whatever was happening to the wide-eyed girl, Mum could take it as a personal affront, as an attack, so rather than supporting she would often attack instead.

One night, Mum's wishes for the end of the wide-eyed girl's relationship with the older man almost came true.

"You're too fat, if you loved me you would lose weight," the new boyfriend announced. The melee that followed was not pleasant, ending in her feeling naked, exposed and humiliated as he pushed her out of the bedroom. She had put on a little weight lately, but as she argued, she was still size twelve, occasionally fourteen.

She had made a mistake. She had relaxed, allowed herself to feel safe. And now that was gone, again.

In its place, the age-old shame reigned supreme once more, and with it a desperate need to protect herself. For him it was a moment, poor expression coming out cruelly, but what she experienced was that once more she was not safe and she was never, ever going to be good enough.

Chapter 23

∽ **Change the Record** ∽

Over the next few months the relationship did not improve. She had joined a barter organisation and was selling more bears now, her confidence in her skill and growing business increasing. It was time to try living on her own again. The idea terrified her, but she needed to try.

She had been working part-time for some months in a fabric shop, and loved it! Her passion for quirky fabric was well satisfied and she loved the staff discount. One day she went into work after missing a shift due to illness, and was surprised when the manager handed her an old LP Record.

Worn looking, it had a dark greyish-black album cover. She took it but did not speak. The "FM" album, the double soundtrack from the film of the same name. She had loved this album so much! During long night shifts on public radio she would play many of its tracks. She was too young to remember the seventies, but for her this album contained the best music of that era.

Problem was, she hadn't seen it for a long time. She turned it over and time froze as she recognised the hand-written label, written by her hand. Her name and the number she had allocated the record were clearly written. Confused, she asked where it came from.

"A strange man brought it in yesterday," the manager said.

"What was strange about him?" she managed to ask, although she already had a fair idea.

"He said this was yours, but he kept his head down, didn't say much else. And his coat, it was just odd. It was a long green coat, and his hair was blondish and messy. He didn't seem like someone you would know."

She didn't stay for the shift. Nausea and fear rose and swam through her body. Tears came fast and continued as she walked home. Her mind raced. He brought this here a few days ago? Is he still here? How did he find her? She sent letters home occasionally, but she never put a return address, and always posted from different suburbs so the postal codes varied. She had been so careful.

"I have to go away for training," the boyfriend announced.

"You can't, don't leave me here alone!" she cried.

"I have to, I can't get out of it. Call your friends, ask one to come and stay with you," he suggested. She wasn't happy, but she did as he asked and a friend was organised. She had convinced the boyfriend to invest in vertical blinds, paying half the cost herself, to help heat the house, she had said. But really, she hated that in the evenings, when it was dark and she could not see out, the many full-length windows and the sliding doors meant that if the Stalker was out there, he could see in.

So the boyfriend went away, the blinds were installed the day he left, and a friend came to stay. But having another female stay didn't help her confidence. Her father called.

"I'm fine," she said, but her voice said otherwise.

"You're not, you sound scared, what the hell's going on?" Dad insisted. She told him about the record, the boyfriend being away, and her terrible sense of foreboding.

"Don't worry," Dad said, "I'll come." Dad couldn't fly, but he did send her brother. She drove to the airport to get him, so excited he was coming that she forgot to be afraid. He laughed heartily as she drove. Did she know what Dad had to go through to get him on that plane? He was short of cash so had to beg Mum! They hadn't even spoken in ages. She gave him a pretty hard time, but she did give him the money.

They talked of all sorts of things. She came to life, feeling a surprising sense of peace having her brother with her. She had been terrible to him when he was young, her behaviour fuelled by jealousy. He had been the surprise baby.

"He only got through because I changed brands of the pill," Mum would say. And Mum adored him. Once he arrived, the large baby boy who cried if anyone other than Mum held him, stole Mum's heart and there seemed little room for anyone else. And now, grown up and laughing at her for the trouble she had caused their father, she felt annoyed that he did not believe her, but more than anything she loved him and was just terribly grateful he was there.

Late that night it began. Noises outside. It sounded like someone was trying to jimmy open the sliding glass windows. It wasn't hard. She had learned how to do that herself on the occasions she had locked herself out of the house. But she had thought about that and cut pieces of thick wooden dowel and placed them in the running track of each window. No matter how the windows jiggled she knew they would not slide open. Anyone wanting to get into that house without permission would have to lift the windows out of their frame or smash them. Either way that gave her plenty of time to run or hide.

When the noise came from the window outside her bedroom her flesh tingled on high alert. In a moment she had run to the back of the house where her brother lay sleeping. Before she said a word, his voice whispered urgently, "Call the bloody police!"

She did, but when a voice answered her call she could not speak. Fear had taken control of her body. The voice on the other end of the phone waited patiently, prompting her gently. Through tears and hiccoughing breaths, she managed to explain what was happening and give her address.

"Stay inside and make sure all the doors and windows are locked," she was instructed. Then the voice was gone. Together they did just that.

Her hands trembled. It took every bit of courage she could muster to pull back the blinds and check all the window locks. They were all locked, she had seen to it herself earlier that day. But once the police told her to check, she could not breathe freely until she had. Just in case she had missed one.

The house was such an open design, even though the blinds were in place and there were no longer exposed windows, she felt exposed, like a sitting duck. Sam the cat was inside with her, wrapping his large, warm, beautiful silver tabby body around her legs. At least he was safe. Her brother made them coffee and they waited. When the police came she was too frightened to open the door. They knocked again, announcing themselves loudly. They searched the house, the property, the garage.

"Are you sure he's not in there?" she questioned, "please don't leave me here with him."

"It's well locked, we've looked in, there's no one there. We suggest you go back to bed. If you hear anything, call us again." And they were gone.

Decades later she was finally able to recognise how much fear had dictated her ability to make good decisions, how terribly it had tainted all that she perceived, of herself as well as others.

Understanding, pure knowing of your own being, your nature, your truth, diminishes the space for reactivity, negativity, cruelty, cruelty to self and others.

Cruelty comes in many disguises, negative self-talk, speaking harshly, fighting, holding self and others in limiting or negative beliefs, not allowing the flow of growth, development and increasing awareness.

A light cannot be made brighter by focusing on the darkness around it. Focusing on the light increases the light, thereby diminishing the darkness.

You can feel your way through the darkness, like a blind man left to find his way out of a deep cave. Feeling, slipping, missing your footing, crying out, cursing, feeling abandoned, afraid and lacking hope.

Try again now, focusing on the tiny little bead of light. Focus completely on the light. Ask the light, what do you need from me to grow stronger, brighter? Be willing to go where the light leads.

The analogy of a lighthouse is so often used in spiritual work. Be a lighthouse, call others to the light so they may recognise their own light. And yet a lighthouse in your terms is not a beacon but a tool to ward off, to warn against perilous conditions that may harm you.

So don't be a lighthouse, don't live in that state of believing you need protection from all the evils of life. Be a star, a bright star, that guides, shows the way, at least for you. A star, light, bright, free, inspiring, admired.

To be truly light is to be free of the fear, free of fear of what negative occurrences might arise, the big "what ifs." To be a lighthouse, on the other hand, is to stand solid in defence of the many dangers you believe surround you in life, and to believe in those dangers so firmly that you use your light to warn others away, so they too might be safe.

Would you rather spend your life stuck in your lighthouse, solid, non-expansive? Or would you choose to be the light in the night sky that gently guides, offers hope and encourages exploration of the universe, within and outside of yourself?

Chapter 24

∽ **Flowers** ∽

Standing on the back verandah, looking out over the yard as they smoked cigarettes, brother and sister spoke casually in an effort to return to normalcy.

"Late for you," came the neighbour's voice from next door. Looking over she saw him, recognised the fat cigarette he was smoking, his durry he called it, and smiled as he introduced a woman. Introductions out of the way, the four chatted until cigarettes were done. She and the brother returned to their beds, the neighbour to very noisy entertaining of his visitor.

The next morning there were people next door, a fair bit of coming and going. What's happening? He's dead, seems to have had a heart attack in the night. But it was only a matter of hours since she had seen him, spoken with him. They had only begun talking a few months back. He would invite her in for a coffee sometimes. They didn't know each other well, but she was saddened by his sudden passing.

After her brother said goodbye, she began looking for somewhere to live. She didn't want to live with someone, but was afraid to live alone. A good compromise was found, a studio under a house. The family, gregarious Hungarian grandparents, lived upstairs, so she wouldn't really be alone. And she wasn't! They were very friendly, supportive and generous with coffee and food! The rent wasn't high, so she was able to get by.

The boyfriend didn't take her move well. Phone calls, letters, baskets of fruit and flowers. She began to fear him. He did not know her full story, so didn't understand that his efforts to appeal to her heart, to win her back, terrified her and pushed her farther away.

During those brief months she had a short fling, discovering once more how awful it felt to be used for sex. Only she hadn't seen it for what it was, she had thought there was at least friendship. Another friend had supported her through this time. He was funny, had an odd sense of humour. She loved how she felt when he smiled. He would come to spend the evening with her, video player under one arm and a bag of videos and snacks under the other.

She loved his company! Loved that they could spend the night stretched out on her bed, as she had no couch, and he made no move to kiss her or seduce her in any way. Sometimes he would pull her into his arms, let her feel his warmth and strength, and she liked this. This was more seductive than he could ever have known.

She told him her secrets, he told her his. There was no rush, just a gentle getting to know each other. This was not something she had experienced before. She was also discovering an ability to be disciplined that she had not recognised in herself before.

She rose early, cut, trimmed the fake fur fabric, vacuumed and got ready to sew teddy bears together before the sun even rose. She felt a bit braver in this new space. Hearing people above her, she didn't feel so vulnerable. She even let Sam out during the day. The landlord's grandchildren loved him!

"I'm going to Tasmania for a surfing holiday," her friend announced, "then I'm coming back to Melbourne to work hard, take on extra jobs and save to get my kids." He was so driven by his need to see his children. She could see and sense his pain and his pride in them whenever he spoke of them. She hadn't been able to meet them though, as they lived with their mother in the UK.

"Why don't you come with me? Could be fun?" he asked, giving her his best cheeky smile. She had a fair idea of what he meant by fun, and yes, it certainly could be! But she had rent to pay, and new clients waiting for delivery of bears she hadn't made yet. She wasn't keen on a trip to Tasmania either, so after a few days of considering, she decided to stay in Melbourne.

"Since you don't want to go, would you mind if a friend went with me?" he had asked. She might, stirrings of jealousy arose, until he explained, "her daughters not long moved back in with her, it would be a good trip for them together."

"Yes," she agreed, as he explained, "it probably would. Sure, sounds great."

In the weeks before his departure she received more attention from the ex-boyfriend. She was already joined in her heart with her gentle friend, so she could not go back.

"Perhaps your ex needs to feel he is the one choosing to end the relationship," a well-meaning friend suggested. And she should know, her husband was a psychiatrist and had seen a lot of this sort of behaviour.

"And you know he really isn't coping," she said, "are you sure you don't want to go back?"

She didn't. But she didn't want to stay feeling afraid, either. It wasn't his fault, he was just trying to save a relationship, having no understanding that she was increasingly terrified with each demand, each phone call or floral tribute that arrived.

Not knowing what else to do, she hatched a plan. Her friend/boyfriend went on the holiday. She agreed to move back into the ex-boyfriend's house, on a trial basis, hoping if she behaved badly enough he would ask her to leave and would then accept the end of their relationship. She would work during the day from her studio room and come home in the evening. He was so pleased she had returned, "What shall we do for the Anzac weekend? Let's make it special."

"Let's drive to Sydney to see my grandparents," she said, "we can stay with my uncle." By the time we've driven all the way there and back, surely he will be glad to see the back of me?

The drive was quite interesting, not like the time she had driven in the heat, her jaw locked shut, on her way to her first commercial radio job in Lismore. Somewhere on that drive they stopped and looked at antiques, and antique rings. He wanted to buy her one, and she almost allowed it. An engagement ring, oh no! No ring, no engagement. This was going to be harder than she thought.

They spent the weekend with her uncle, had dinner with her grandmother, and began the drive home. Stopping at a roadside café for coffee, she answered a call from Mum, who was demanding to know where she was.

"Heading home to Melbourne, we've been in Sydney," she responded. Mum was furious!

"You can't spend the rest of your life with him, what do you think you're doing?" Mum ranted. It was a brief conversation. Mum was right, even if her expression of it was harsh. But she couldn't explain what she was doing just now.

He seemed to be reaching the end of his patience with her, his temper shorter than he would have liked. She was watching the sky as they drove south, toward Melbourne. In it she saw the strangest cloud formation. It looked like a huge, grey, broad arrow. The broad arrow that had marked the clothing of convicts in Tasmania. She felt it pulling her homeward. Felt the urgency to get home, but they had some hours to drive yet.

Unease seeped through her. She had no idea why, but the arrow in the sky had left her quiet, contemplative. Perhaps her discomfort just came from the fact that she was in a relationship she didn't want to be in, waiting to be released.

She hadn't heard from her friend. Where was he? When was he coming home? She missed him. They got home late in the night. He poured himself a drink and turned on the television.

"Shit! Come and look at this!" he exclaimed.

Both sat perched on the edge of the couch, straining forward to see what their minds could not believe. A massacre? In Tasmania? Today? The news broadcast went on for hours, updating as information came in. It was hard to watch, but impossible not to. In lounge rooms around the world countless others no doubt did the same.

That afternoon, at the Port Arthur Historic Site in Tasmania, a gunman had shot approximately fifty people. The exact figures weren't known yet, but it was believed thirty-five of the victims were deceased. As the horror of this settled in, there was the uncomfortable question of where her friend was. She was not willing to contemplate that he could have been there.

The next day was her friend's birthday. She'd like to call him, message him at least. But he didn't respond to her calls. Their mutual friend called.

"Have you been able to get a hold of him? We have called and called and there's no answer." She sat on the edge of the bed, body light and faint, and cried. "No," she spluttered, "I haven't. I just can't believe it's possible he was there. He can't be."

They agreed she would make some phone calls. She called the helpline, no they said, no one of that description. An hour later she called again. In a moment of inspiration, she was able to describe the tattoo, a family crest her friend had designed himself, on his upper arm. The line went deadly silent.

The chasm of fear opened up and swallowed her whole. Eventually the voice spoke once more.

"Yes, we do have a man matching that description." A pause, the wide-eyed girl asked the question she didn't want to hear the answer to.

"Is he alive?"

"Yes, he's been taken to hospital." Calling their mutual friend, she struggled to maintain her voice, to speak, but managed to tell him everything she had been told.

"I can help with money if you need it," he said, "but you have to go. One of us has to go, I can't get away from work because we're already short because he's not here. I'm so sorry, can you go?"

"Yes, yes, I can." And she did. The next day she flew to Hobart, every part of her dreading what she might find, and her spirit willing him to hold on until she got there.

The thought of him dying, alone in a strange place, was heartbreaking.

Chapter 25

~ Eye of the Storm ~

Arriving at Hobart Airport late at night, she was glad of her mother's partner's generous offer to collect her. He took her straight to the hospital. It was late, but time didn't seem important. He walked in with her, silently offering his support and strength as they looked for her friend.

First they had to make their way through the media pack outside the main entrance to the hospital. She had done a year of nursing training here nine years ago, but in her distressed state she could not remember if there was another entrance the press might not know about. They were everywhere, like swarming locusts. Bright lights set up, people being interviewed. Security was visible and tense. Why now, she wondered, isn't the danger over now?

As she moved towards reception to ask for her friend's whereabouts, she became aware of a female journalist who had somehow gotten past the security, and was listening to her words. The journalist's presence, pushing into her terrified space, amplified her anguish. Mum's partner stepped in behind the wide-eyed girl, then started stepping backwards. The journalist had to back off now, or be stepped on.

He stayed with her thus as they moved through the hospital. Thankfully, security was not allowing members of the press beyond the reception area. Once they were in the lift and on their way they were free of prying eyes, microphones and cameras.

His deep blue eyes filled with tears of compassion for this man he did not know, his face screwed up with the intensity of his emotions.

Looking from the doorway they could see the man in the bed before them was attached to a number of machines. His face and upper body were bloodied and swollen. It was hard to imagine what horrors he might have experienced.

She stepped forward, into the room. Hesitating, for a moment.

Was it right that she was here? Is this what he would want? Their mutual friend had thought as she did, that she needed to be there for him, at least one familiar face in a world of hurt.

As she contemplated the man who lay before her, he opened one eye. Just a little, then the other.

In the next moment her heart shattered. His wounded, beautiful face, so changed in this swollen and damaged state, smiled at her.

A brief, life-changing smile.

She walked to his bed, blowing him a kiss through her tears.

"I've brought your kids to see you," she said quietly, small voice trembling as she placed a framed photo of his children where he could see it.

She touched the hand on the bed lightly, it was at least as swollen as his face, the normally strong fingers looking so large and puffy, not like his at all. His eyes closed once more, and she left.

Tired and emotional, she reached her mother's house and collapsed in tears as they comforted her, made her coffee then bade her sleep. The next morning Mum went to work as usual, while her partner drove the wide-eyed girl to the hospital. Her friend was conscious momentarily during her visit. He would be asleep for some time, a nurse explained. The next twenty-four hours are critical. There are a few things we need to do for him, why don't you go and have a coffee, come back in an hour or so?

She wandered through the city streets, then to her mother's office. Mum had opened her own business, a secretarial service, where she worked on her own. The wide-eyed girl made them both coffee, then sat down to sip at hers. Her thoughts and emotions swirled like a frantic whirlpool.

What if he didn't pull through? She didn't want to imagine her world without him, whatever the nature of their relationship would be after this. She tried her best to pull herself together and answer Mum's questions, but she didn't feel comfortable with the tone.

"Why are you so upset?" Mum yelled angrily, her face going red. "Who the hell is he anyway?"

"He's my friend, Mum. And he might die, today, tomorrow. His jaw is shattered, he's got a bloody great hole in the side of his neck, and a little bit of flesh or shattered bone might get into his blood and take him out at any moment." She sat down, shaking from the effort of trying to explain, breathe and cry all at once.

Mum was really yelling now, her voice high and nasty.

"I've never heard of him! If he's your friend why don't I know?" Mum demanded.

She gathered the remnants of her voice and answered, "Mum, we don't live in the same state. I don't know all your friends. Does it matter? We've been seeing each other for a little while. It hadn't gotten too serious. You would have met him," her voice trailed off.

Head down, she sobbed and struggled for breath, looking up as her mother's voice reached her once more. Mum's face seemed to wobble as she yelled.

"What kind of daughter are you that I have to find out about this friend second-hand?" The wide-eyed girl didn't have the energy for this.

"Mum," she said as she reached for her bag and stood up, "I called you first, as soon as I knew, and here I am now, with you. What more can I do?" As she walked out of the office she could hear her mother's irrational name-calling and ranting fading out in the background.

Crying again, she didn't even try to stop the tears as she made her way to the hire car company. She would need a car to get from Dad's to the hospital every day. The nurse had said her friend's mother was arriving tomorrow too, she might need transport or somewhere to stay.

Once the car was organised she drove to Dad's. He made no demands, just made a coffee, sat down and listened.

"You can stay here," he offered.

"Thanks, I was hoping you'd say that," she replied, tears streaming once more. She had seen her face in the mirror at the hire car place and it was a bit of a shock to her. Her face was so pale, eyes swollen, pupils barely visible.

"I won't tell anyone you're here if that helps, I don't think you need any extra drama," Dad offered. She cried more, tears of gratitude.

"Thanks Dad," was all she could say. He made more coffee.

Back at the hospital she sat quietly, watching him breathe, listened to the machines monitoring and assisting him, and it hit her. There was absolutely nothing she could do. Here in this building, with its grey floor tiles, mundane décor and nothing familiar to inspire him, he might die, any moment. She had been there for some time in quiet contemplation, just watching him, willing him to live, when a nurse came in, standing beside her.

"There's no easy way to say this, but family have arrived and they want you to go," the nurse informed her. Panic rose in her, making her feel dizzy as she stood to look at the door. An older couple stood there, waiting for her to leave.

Who were they? He had spoken about an aunt and uncle who lived in Melbourne, but he hadn't seen them for some time. She looked back at his swollen face, promising silently she would be back.

"Who are they?" she asked the nurse, "what right do they have?"

"They are his aunt and uncle, they are the closest living relatives, so they have the say. I am so sorry, there really is nothing I can do. They know he might not survive the coming hours and don't know you, so they won't have you here."

Chapter 26

Stay

Leaving the ward she found a phone box near the main entrance and called their friend in Melbourne. Feeling a little panicky, unsure of what she should do, she relayed the events to him as best she could.

"Don't give up, he needs you there," he encouraged her. "You are the one he would want there, just stay. I can't come, it has to be you."

Feeling supported, better for hearing her friend's voice, she agreed. As she turned away from the phone an extended camera lens hit her in the eye. A female reporter backed off, fast, looked at her sideways, then took off out of the main entrance doors. She had seen that reporter the night she arrived, and this morning. The woman was unstoppable! Had she heard her conversation? Would it be plastered over the papers within hours? That was too much for her to even imagine dealing with right now.

Back to Dad's for a while. A rest.

"Go back later," Dad suggested, "if they're older folk, they'll be wanting a rest themselves before long."

Once rested, fed and filled up on enough of Dad's coffee to keep her awake forever, she headed back into the hospital a little after ten that night. Dad was right! She made her way to his ward, into his room, without interference. There was no one to be seen.

Quietly she sat in the chair beside his bed, watching him sleep. She stayed for some time, before quietly heading home to her father's. Nurses came and went, but did not disturb her or ask her to leave.

She woke early, returning to the hospital. Nursing staff were tending to him. She smiled, grateful for their kindness. One had brought her a cup of tea, placing it on a little table beside her. Thanking her, she understood that she needed to drink it and go. It would not do for the relatives to return and find her there. She could not think about them without feeling great resentment. They at least could have asked her who she was, given her an opportunity to explain, but they didn't.

"If I were them, I would be so glad he had a friend who loved him enough to be here," she said later to her sister as she sat in her lounge room trying to act "normal" while feeling anything but.

"You shouldn't demonize Martin Bryant, who knows what his life was like for him to do something like this," her sister's partner lectured. He was making yet another coffee, for which she was very grateful, but his words were hard to ignore.

"Go to the hospital," she replied, "go and talk with the man who had part of his arm shot off, talk to the ones who were injured, talk to people whose family have died."

Her sister's lounge room was quite small, even more so by the presence of at least four adults, including her sister, who was nursing her young baby. The wide-eyed girl began to disappear from the conversation, focusing on her beautiful niece, the dear little face that to her looked a little elfin. Translucent skin, fine ginger-blonde hair, tiny fingers that curled around hers and held on tight. If her suspicions about the gunman were correct, this gorgeous little being would be safe now, no fear of attack from an unseen assailant.

Tears rolled thick and fast as the debate continued around her.

"It'll be alright, he'll pull through," her sister encouraged, hugging her.

Later that day she went back to the hospital, and finding him alone, sat with him awhile. She had seen the relatives in the café downstairs, just sitting down with their cups of tea, so she guessed she had at least fifteen minutes. Senses on high alert, she heard them coming. Gathering her bag, she quickly made her exit, putting her head down as she moved into the hallway.

There were more of them now. Looking up, she saw the compassionate blue eyes of the woman she knew to be his mother, and one of his sisters beside her.

Their faces said it all. Tired, fearful and so sad. They had travelled a long way to be with him. She watched as their expressions froze in the moment they saw him. A moment she understood only too well. That moment when the eyes have seen what the heart could not, did not want to comprehend, but now it is seen cannot be denied. The genie is out of the bottle, the horror is real, and now must be dealt with.

The moment was so brief, replaced by such deep compassion she felt their pain in her own body. Tears threatened, the lump rising in her throat made it hard to swallow and her chest felt tight and painful. Head down, she left once more.

Other family members arrived. The children in the photo frame, chaperoned by their mother and his brother. What a powerful moment it had been. Seeing this man, much more stocky in build, a shock of dark hair, solid set jaw and an incredibly emotional face, had taken her breath away. He did not look like her friend, not on the surface, but his eyes told her who he was. Tearful, emotional, vocal. Their eyes met as they passed in the corridor and she felt his passion and his pain for his family.

Time passed as though in a vacuum. She visited when no one else was there. In-between visits she spent a little time with his friend, who had travelled to Port Arthur in her place. She was badly injured, but in better physical shape than he was. This small woman had not only witnessed the carnage in the café and been injured herself, but had witnessed the killing of her teenaged daughter. The wide-eyed girl was beyond words. She could only imagine how this friend of her friend must be feeling.

Finally, she introduced herself to the English family. They were kinder, more accepting of her than she had expected. The brother, whom she had recognised by his eyes, encouraged her to stay. She ran errands, offered to take anyone who needed time out for a drive, to see a little of Hobart. They weren't visiting for long though, so spent every moment they could with her friend. Tearfully, she explained to the brother what had happened, why she could not be in the room. By now her friend was able to communicate, talking a little and writing.

"I'll ask him," said the brother, "he can say whether or not you should be here." Nervously, she agreed.

What if she had got it all wrong and he didn't want her here? But she agreed. Ask him. The brother emerged from the hospital room grinning widely, arm extended to her.

"He said yes!"

As her friend's condition began to stabilise he began asking about going home to Melbourne. The doctors encouraged a longer stay in Hobart, but they hadn't counted on his enthusiasm to get as far away from Hobart as he could.

"Melbourne is home, I will heal better there," he insisted. The immediate family had returned to the UK, amidst much hugging, crying and promising by all to keep in touch.

She wanted to beg his mother to stay, please don't leave us, but it didn't feel right to do that. As frightened as she was, she promised.

"I will look after him. I wish you didn't have to go," she said to his mother.

"Me too," his beautiful mother replied quietly through her tears, "look after him."

Her heart broke for them all. She could only imagine how hard it must have been for them to leave while he was still so unwell.

Chapter 27

❦ Adjusting ❦

Returning to Melbourne after the drama and intensity of Hobart was surreal. Their mutual friend collected her from the airport, wanting to know all she could tell him. There were many tears shared as she tried to explain the feelings, raw emotions experienced by her, her friend, his family, other survivors.

She remembered the awful moment, helping to sort out the belongings in her friend's car in Hobart so his friend's and her deceased daughter's belongings could be taken home. The clothing of a teenager, a soft toy the girl had collected in their travels. She remembered how sick she had felt, helping her uncle in this, surprised by how much emotion she could feel for a girl she would now never meet.

Wanting to comfort the uncle, a friend, but not having any words that might help. All they could do, together with his friend who had travelled with him to help him, was complete their miserable task, allow the emotions to surface and flow. The car would be driven back to Melbourne on the boat, for it would be a long time before her friend would be able to drive it again.

Those first few hours home in Melbourne, she could almost have believed none of it was real. She went to her bedsit under the Hungarians' house and sat, clutching a hot cup of coffee in her hands. She could feel the steel of the door frame digging into her rump as she sat in her doorway, looking out into her landlord's yard and feeling the warmth of the sun welcome her home. Coffee smelled good.

There was a blissful moment where no one required her to talk or explain, she could just be. There were many different plants in this yard, many not in bloom as it was getting cold in the journey into winter. She admired the shine on the leaves of bush near her door, like little green mirrors. And then the moment was gone. It hadn't lasted long, but it was delicious.

She could escape for a moment, pretend none of the horror was real. How must it be for him? With the pain of his injuries, the loss of his friend's daughter, he could not escape that cruel reality for a second.

Sitting with him late into the evening as he settled into his new surroundings in a Melbourne hospital, she was surprised at how casual the staff seemed. It worried her that the nurses didn't seem to be checking on him anywhere near as often as the Hobart nurses had. It would be some time before she realised that here, although the care provided was just as thorough, these staff had not been caught up in the full horror of the massacre.

They had not been in the hospital that Sunday afternoon as the casualties began to arrive, knowing as they met them that the massacre might continue as the gunman was still at large. Nor had they seen the state in which he had arrived, desperate to live but not sure if his body would allow it. A huge, bloody hole where the flesh of his neck should have been, countless fractures to his handsome jaw, blood everywhere. His survival a story in itself, but his to tell.

Here, instead of evicting her, the hospital staff provided cushions and a blanket. She sat with him as he slept, finding comfort in his breathing.

In the weeks that followed he had more surgery to help his jaw grow back together. Fiercely independent, he was released from hospital with his mouth wired shut and a pair of pliers.

"Why the pliers?" she had asked.

"So if I choke," he mumbled, "you can cut the bloody wires and I can open my mouth."

Ohhh… that was a pretty terrifying prospect! About this time he asked to visit her ex. It was a brief visit, but it was clear to her ex she wouldn't be returning. As a career army soldier, he warned her.

"You know how messed up war veterans can be, this could well be a hell of a lot worse. Are you sure you want to do this? Are you sure you can do this?" he asked.

No, she wasn't sure she could, but she was sure she wanted to.

Imagine living on little boxes of protein drinks, only a few different flavours, and delivered by a straw through the wires that keep your shattered jaw shut. It wasn't long before her friend tired of this regimen.

"Roast, I want a roast!" he cried. How could she deliver that? In hospitals and nursing homes meals were liquified for those who had trouble chewing and swallowing. Why not? And so she and their mutual friend began cooking meals and pulverising them. Imagine a plate with a puddle of green (that's peas), a puddle of greyish brown (roast meat in gravy), an orange puddle that once was carrots and you get the idea. It wasn't fantastic, but it did provide relief from the drinks. The pureed fried eggs and baked beans were less of a hit. The beans apparently were not so bad, but the eggs were not so good.

By now she had packed up her bedsit under the Hungarians' house and moved in with her friend to look after him. Their mutual friend lived there too, so both received support from him and his frequently visiting partner. It was quite a load he carried, with incredible grace and compassion. Many a time he massaged her head and neck while the three of them watched television. His partner, a truly compassionate woman with great empathy, visited often and also provided welcome companionship.

The wide-eyed girl had managed to squeeze her sewing machines and teddy bears into a corner of the spare room. But she had no heart for it. Every time she looked at the bears she was overwhelmed by grief for the girl who had died. What if she had just said yes to his request and gone with him on that trip to Tasmania? Would he even have gone to Port Arthur that day if she had been travelling with him instead?

Many years later when she asked this question, yet again, this is the answer she heard intuitively:

You say to those who ask, I must live life to the fullest, I have to make it extraordinary, to honour them, especially the girl who died in my place. And that makes perfect sense. Logically anyway.

But it isn't extraordinary. It hurts. People around you hurt. No one knows how to live with this, certainly not you. But you do your best, you look after him as best you can. It is a terrifying responsibility. You saw what happened through intuitive connection, and you can't experience his terror, pain, fear, guilt, but you can feel it in him.

There is no training for this, and if there were it would be too late because now you're in it. You always felt there was great terror in this world, but this was beyond the realm of your imagination.

So you judge yourself to be lacking. Not a good enough nurse to him, not quick enough to always know what to do to relieve pain, avoid situations that might bring on post-traumatic conditions, know when to encourage rest and pulling back rather than encouraging his desire to push. And you had so little knowledge then. Imagine how much more you could do now with all that you have learned! As hard as it was, as much as it hurt, you were beginning to observe.

You began to learn detachment in the positive. Detachment from the experience of others so that you may observe and learn before responding, if responding is required at all. No more diving into the deep waters and wondering why you are near drowning. Standing back by the water's edge, observing, gaining understanding, is far more powerful for you and those you are called to assist.

You call this your velcro theory. This is how detachment has different purposes. When detached from your true self you can be so easily caught up in everybody else's business, spending little or no time in self-reflection and meditation. This is not good for you. When detached from everybody else, so you are present and observing but not jumping in on their experiences, not taking them on as your own, you are able to see and do so much more because you are not detached from yourself.

Chapter 28

❦ You Can't Tell Anyone ❦

She went with him to the teenage girl's funeral. She watched the white birds that were released at the graveside, wondering where they went to. Were they free now? Looking at the girl's mother she felt awkward, overwhelmed with grief for them all. And guilt. Survivor's guilt, a counsellor told her.

They hadn't told her how to face it, deal with it, just given it a name. And she felt every ounce of it. Who was she that she should be alive when so many were not? Tears flowed hot and fast for the girl, her mother and the friend she now lived with who stood silently, dressed in the recently, meticulously repaired Driza-bone coat he had been wearing when he was shot.

"You're a dressmaker," he had insisted, "you can repair it."

The Driza-bone company had given him fabric to repair the coat, along with a new coat to replace the damaged one. But he didn't want to wear the new coat. He wanted to wear the damaged one, as a reminder of all that had transpired and his survival against such profound odds. His coat had been cut off him by the paramedics who fought to save his life. Although it had supposedly been washed, it was a long way from clean.

As she trimmed, stitched and repaired the coat, she kept her mouth firmly shut so that she did not breathe in the fragments of crusty dried blood that flew into her face each time the needle hit it.

The process took the best part of a day, requiring a lot of coffee and the shedding of many tears. She had heard the recollections of those who had worked so hard to save her friend's life that day. She could not help but picture him lying on the café floor, blood flowing freely from the horrific neck wound, blood filling his throat and making it difficult for him to breathe. After all he had suffered, she understood his need to repair this coat and felt honoured that she could do this for him. As overwhelmed as she was, she understood that for him, putting the coat back together was playing a part in putting him back together.

Stopping frequently to look out the window, feel the warm sun on her face, she was struck by how calming the sun felt. And yet it was one such sunny Sunday afternoon, 28 April 1996, when the massacre had occurred and all their lives had been irreversibly altered in the most terrible way.

In the back of her mind she wondered, could Martin Bryant be the man who had stalked her for so many years? What if she had tried harder to stop him? If she had allowed her friends to go after him, so long ago, would he have still done this?

So many questions, but no answers. Just overwhelming grief, guilt and shame. Shame that she did not manage to stop him. Shame that she was alive. She felt as though she was drifting alone in a sea of despair, in a life raft with no instructions.

She was afraid to voice her concern. Afraid to be judged, afraid people would say she was crazy.

"You're not crazy," her friend said. "The day before we were shot, we were in Hobart. We went to Salamanca Market. He was there, he was behind me a few times when I looked. I thought he was following me, but I just shrugged it off. But it was him. He had that long greenish coat on. Messy hair."

To think that the Stalker was capable of this massacre terrified her. Her body felt cold, uninhabited. She began chewing relentlessly at her nails.

"I've asked my lawyer to find out what she can," her friend said, "she has some contacts in Tasmania."

Surely not, surely it couldn't be him.

One grey winter's afternoon, some months after their return to Melbourne, they were woken from an afternoon snooze by the phone ringing. Rubbing her face sleepily as she picked up the phone, she was surprised to hear a man's voice asking for her.

"Yes, that's me," she answered warily. The voice introduced himself as a sergeant from Tasmania Police.

"Your lawyer," he explained, "asked me to let you know what we found here. I can't give you any details, but I can confirm that things you listed as stolen from your home by the man who stalked you were found in his home. But you won't find any evidence now."

Everything in her body seemed to come to a halt. Breath, heartbeat. Time slowed as her body slid down the wall she had been leaning on. As she landed, she asked what it was they had found.

"You won't find any evidence of it now, and I never made this phone call," the sergeant advised.

"So it was him? My stalker, it was Martin Bryant? He did this?" she stammered.

"Yes. But you don't need to worry now," the policeman stated, "he has gone away for a very long time, a very long holiday, and he won't be coming back. You're safe now. But you can't tell anyone."

"It was him," she stammered to the boyfriend who had started out as her friend. Awake, listening to her conversation, his handsome face was as pale as she felt.

"All those people, they're all dead, you're hurt, and I'm safe." She had known the truth for some time, felt it so strongly. But she hadn't been prepared for the emotions having it confirmed would unleash.

The horror of it shocked her physically and emotionally. Her chest hurt, ribs felt as if they were bruised. She was painfully, deeply aware of her heart beating, her breath. Eyes wide open, she kept hearing the sergeant's words.

"You don't need to worry, you're safe now. But you can't tell anyone."

Epilogue

December, 2017.

Twenty-one years have passed.

"Ending is oddly abrupt, people need more time to get used to not being on the roller coaster with you," an editor suggested upon assessing the first manuscript of this book.

'But I love the ending," the wide-eyed girl responded passionately, "it's powerful."

Powerful. That was how it had felt in 1996 after that phone call. The policeman's words kept ringing in her head, "You don't need to worry, you're safe now."

She was, but so many weren't. How could she celebrate being alive when thirty-five people had died? Why was she alive? Occasionally she and her partner went to meetings with other survivors, but she was not always made welcome.

"You weren't there, you have no right," one survivor said to her. Harsh words, but they mirrored exactly how she felt.

A well-meaning psychiatrist said to her at their first meeting, "That was many years ago now, why are you still so caught up in it?"

This was terrifying. If even a psychiatrist couldn't help her come to terms with her feelings of grief, guilt and regret, who could?

She went to university to study psychology, surely the answers lay there. Nope. Another dead end. Finally, early in 2012, she discovered a therapy that connected the dots. Everything she had ever felt, experienced emotionally but not allowed herself to express, at least to herself if to no one else, was stored in the tissues of her body. Having been so utterly overwhelmed by trauma, she had never let herself fully express her emotions. She believed they would consume her and she would never be able to function again.

No wonder by 2012 she was more than twenty-five kilos above her ideal weight and lamented two failed marriages!

Sitting at her desk one day in her safe, well-paying government job, she received a phone call that set her free. For some months she had been unhappy in her job, but had not had the courage to leave it.

"Hallo Karen, I can see you. I am watching you. I can see everything you do. Are you enjoying that sandwich?"

Just like that, she was flung back into the emotions of terror, not knowing when or how Martin would strike next. Frozen, it seemed an eternity before she could hang up the phone. Once disconnected, she tore the headset off her head and stood up. Pacing around her office space. She couldn't stand still, it wasn't safe to be still. She was a sitting duck!

Again!

Her entire body trembled. She looked to the windows to see if he was there, fully expecting to see Martin staring back at her.

People started to notice something was wrong. One woman put an arm around her, guiding her to a seat. The phone rang again. Tears fell fast, unbidden. Hiding her face with her hands, she felt embarrassed but could not stop the flow of emotion.

The caller turned out to be a prank, a team member from another office.

"He was calling Karen in Sydney," the woman comforting her explained, "he just dialled the wrong number."

The explanation didn't matter. His work was done. Once she recovered from the shock and her body stopped shaking enough for her to talk clearly, she walked over to her supervisor and announced she needed to resign. An understanding man, he replied, "You have holidays due, perhaps today should be your last day?"

And so it was.

Supporting herself in the first few years that followed wasn't easy. The wide-eyed girl attended training after training, determined to discover the core reason for her behaviours and life choices. She felt ashamed still, but as her understanding grew, the shame began to dissolve.

To her surprise, she discovered she was a highly intuitive being! Many times she had begun exploration of intuition, but it wasn't until she began to allow herself to feel and really express her deepest, darkest emotions and memories that her intuition really kicked in.

It occurred to her that the stories, the events that had caused her so much pain, were just stories. She didn't have to stay there anymore, trapped in the moment. Her teachers from this time would likely tell you that's exactly what they were teaching, but it wasn't until she really got it for herself that change really began.

Slowly she unraveled the events, many her own decisions, that had increased the shame. In 2017, at a writer's retreat in Hawaii, the last piece of the shame puzzle finally dropped into place. The shame, which came from extreme fear following the sexual assault against her when she was a child, had never left. She had lived her entire life in fear. All of her decisions had been based on fear.

Then she would look back at past decisions and ask herself, "How could I have done that? Why didn't I stand up for myself? Why did I leave the cat with him?"

And finally, thanks to the years of learning before reaching that pivotal moment in Hawaii, she got it. She was terrified, always terrified. But she covered it so well with bravado, humour and apparent confidence that very few had seen through it.

But she does. And now she is free to say goodbye to the shame, goodbye to the guilt, goodbye to the terror. There are moments when memories are triggered, moments when she is overwhelmed with emotion. But she lets the emotions flow now, without judgment.

She is free to reach for the stars and live openly, fully and joyfully.

Appendix

The journey from shame and guilt to living joyfully began with Psychosomatic Therapy, under the tutelage of Hobart-based teacher, Vicki Delpero. Vicki was teaching the work of Hermann Müller, creator of Psychosomatic Therapy. Becoming Vicki's assistant, I travelled the country with her and continued learning and allowing the recognition and release of trauma from my body and soul.

This was how I began to understand the part I had played in every aspect of my life, and how to move from being a victim to just being me. I also learned bodywork techniques designed to release trapped emotions from the body.

Thus began my understanding that touch wasn't just about someone else wanting sex! Vicki's work has evolved greatly since then and I highly recommend her Soul Embodiment training.

www.soulembodiment.com.au

Six months after first studying with Vicki I began learning to be comfortable with the human body, with my body, by attending Kahuna Massage training with Mette Sorensen, at Mette's Institute, Kin Kin, Queensland. Although at first I was incredibly reluctant, terrified and incredibly awkward, the training was beautiful. It wasn't just the training, but the community I became a part of too. A community of people whose goal is to build love in the world by offering healing massage in a sacred space of honouring body and soul.

www.mettesinstitute.com.au/

In 2013 I spent a week with Hermann and Marie Müller, completing advanced Psychosomatic Therapy training. I bared my soul to Hermann, spoke my terrifying truth. He held me with his incredible gaze and listened. I sobbed, struggled and was fearful he might not believe, he might think me mad. But Hermann saw me, believed me and understood me. Hermann then shared his understanding of my experiences with Martin Bryant. Thus began my journey of daring to share my truth. I owe immeasurable thanks to Hermann for that life changing moment.

http://www.psychosomatictherapycollege.com.au/

The last eighteen months have been a fabulous journey of learning with Rachael Jayne and Datta Groover. This dynamic duo have been helping me find my voice, learning to speak on stage without being totally disabled by fear and doubt, and to establish my dream business. Two businesses really. One is writing and editing, the other is establishing Rainbow Animal Sanctuary in Tasmania, Australia.

www.rachaeljayne.com

The Groovers also introduced me to Tom Bird, whose writing workshop I attended in May, 2017. I was finally able to begin writing this book from my heart, not my head! If you feel compelled to write, but it just doesn't work for you, I heartily recommend Tom's workshop. It worked magic for me!

www.tombird.com

And thanks to each of these amazing teachers, I finally have the courage to offer my editing skills for other writers who are discovering they have the courage to share their voice, their truth.

www.karencollyer.com

Many teachers and friends have helped me in my healing journey of discovery. I have mentioned Vicki, Mette and Hermann because their teaching and guidance in the first two years were pivotal for me, creating the dramatic shifts that have allowed all else to follow.

In the early days there were friends who provided company, friends who talked me through the late nights where I thought I could not make it, friends who made me laugh and see the beauty in myself when I couldn't. What these beautiful friends have taught me is the importance of community, gratitude and just how strong and capable I truly am.

There are too many to name. They know who they are, and they know I love them with every ounce of my being.

Whatever your journey, I wish you well and honour you for allowing me to share mine with you.

Karen, the wide-eyed girl.

www.ingramcontent.com/pod-product-compliance
Lightning Source LLC
Chambersburg PA
CBHW030524080526
44586CB00011B/306